THE

ULTIMATE

PLANT BASED

DIET

COOKBOOK

TAKE CARE OF YOUR HEALTH WITH NATURAL FOODS

-WHITNEY HAYES-

TABLE OF CONTENTS:

CHAPTER 1: BREAKFAST RECIPES

Poppy Seed Bundt Cake

Prep:
30 mins
Cook:
1 hr
Total:
1 hr 30 mins
Servings:
12
Yield:
1 - 10 inch bundt pan

INGREDIENTS:

4 eggs
1 teaspoon vanilla extract
2 ½ cups all-purpose flour
1 teaspoon baking soda
½ teaspoon salt
1 ½ tablespoons ground cinnamon
½ cup white sugar
¼ cup poppy seeds
1 cup buttermilk
1 cup butter
1 ½ cups white sugar

DIRECTIONS:

1

Preheat oven to 350 degrees F (175 degrees C), grease a 10 inch bundt pan. Mix together cinnamon and 1/2 cup sugar. Sprinkle part of the cinnamon sugar mixture evenly over greased pan. This will form a thin crust over the cake. Set aside the remaining cinnamon sugar mixture.

2

Soak poppy seed in buttermilk for 6 to 8 hours or overnight. Cream butter and 1 1/2 cup sugar until light and fluffy. Add eggs one at a time, beating well after each addition. Add vanilla.

3

Sift flour, salt and soda together. Add to butter mixture alternately with the poppy seed mixture. Blend well.

4

Put the batter in the pan in layers, sprinkling the reserved cinnamon sugar mixture between each layer. If you spread your batter thin, you should get three layers of cinnamon sugar.

5

Bake at 350 degrees F (175 degrees C) for 50 minutes or until a toothpick inserted comes out clean. Set cake on rack to cool for one hour.

NUTRITION FACTS:

410 calories; protein 6.2g; carbohydrates 55.7g; fat 18.7g;

Cauliflower Hash Browns

Prep:
15 mins
Cook:
10 mins
Total:
25 mins
Servings:
4
Yield:
4 hash brown cakes

INGREDIENTS:

¾ teaspoon salt
¼ teaspoon ground black pepper
¼ teaspoon smoked paprika
1 tablespoon extra-virgin olive oil
½ head cauliflower, grated
½ cup shredded extra-sharp Cheddar cheese
1 large egg, beaten
¼ cup panko bread crumbs
⅛ cup chopped green onion

DIRECTIONS:

1

Place grated cauliflower, Cheddar cheese, egg, panko, green onion, salt, pepper, and paprika in a large bowl. Mix until combined; mixture will be very crumbly.

2

Heat olive oil in a large skillet over medium-high heat until hot. Scoop up some of the cauliflower mixture using an ice cream scoop; pat into a flat patty. Gently place patty in the hot oil; reduce heat to medium. Repeat with remaining mixture. Cook until a golden brown crust forms, about 5 minutes per side. Remove to a platter and serve immediately.

NUTRITION FACTS:

140 calories; protein 7.3g; carbohydrates 9.5g; fat 9.4g;

Pistachio Cake

Prep:

20 mins

Cook:

50 mins

Additional:

5 mins

Total:

1 hr 15 mins

Servings:

14

Yield:

1 - 10 inch tube pan

INGREDIENTS:

1 ½ cups water

¼ cup vegetable oil

½ teaspoon almond extract

7 drops green food coloring

1 (18.25 ounce) package yellow cake mix

1 (3.4 ounce) package instant pistachio pudding mix

4 eggs

DIRECTIONS:

1

Preheat oven to 350 degrees F (175 degrees C). Grease and flour a 10 inch tube pan.

2

In a large bowl mix together cake mix and pudding mix. Make a well in the center and pour in eggs, water, oil, almond extract and green food coloring. Blend ingredients, then beat for 2 minutes at medium speed.

3

Pour into prepared 10 inch tube pan. Bake in the preheated oven for 50 to 55 minutes, or until cake springs back when lightly pressed. Cool in pan 15 minutes. Turn out onto a wire rack and cool completely.

NUTRITION FACTS:

242 calories; protein 3.4g; carbohydrates 35.2g; fat 9.8g;

Eggplant Panini

Prep:
15 mins
Cook:
15 mins
Total:
30 mins
Servings:
4
Yield:
4 servings

INGREDIENTS:

½ (12 ounce) jar roasted red bell peppers, drained and sliced
4 ounces shredded mozzarella cheese
¼ cup roasted garlic hummus
1 baby eggplant, cut into
1/4-inch slices
salt and ground black pepper to taste
¼ cup olive oil, divided
1 loaf flat bread, sliced horizontally and cut into 4 equal pieces

DIRECTIONS:

1
Season eggplant slices with salt and pepper; let stand for 2 minutes.

2
Heat 2 tablespoons olive oil in a skillet over medium-high heat; saute
1/2 of the eggplant until golden brown, 2 to 3 minutes per side.
Repeat with remaining olive oil and eggplant.

3

Preheat a panini press according to manufacturer's instructions.

4

Layer eggplant, roasted red pepper, and mozzarella cheese, respectively, onto the bottom piece of each flat bread. Spread 1 tablespoon hummus on the inside of each top piece of flat bread and place over the mozzarella layer, creating a panini.

5

Grill each panini on the preheated panini press until cooked through and cheese is melted, about 7 minutes.

NUTRITION FACTS:

401 calories; protein 15.7g; carbohydrates 41.5g; fat 21.7g;

Vegetarian Bolognese with Soy Chorizo

Prep:

10 mins

Cook:

15 mins

Total:

25 mins

Servings:

8

Yield:

8 servings

INGREDIENTS:

1 teaspoon dried oregano

½ teaspoon cayenne pepper

½ teaspoon paprika

2 teaspoons chopped fresh basil

½ teaspoon freshly ground black pepper

fine sea salt to taste

3 cups water

1 (16 ounce) package thin spaghetti

1 tablespoon olive oil

18 ounces marinara sauce

1 (14.5 ounce) can diced tomatoes

12 ounces soy chorizo

DIRECTIONS:

1

Bring about 3 cups lightly salted water to a boil in a medium-sized pot. Add pasta and cook, stirring occasionally, until tender yet firm to the bite, about 11 minutes.

2

Meanwhile, heat olive oil over medium heat in a large skillet. Add marinara sauce and diced tomatoes and stir. Add soy chorizo and mix until texture is even, 3 to 5 minutes. Add oregano, cayenne pepper, and paprika; reduce heat and simmer until pasta has finished cooking, about 8 minutes more. Add basil.

3

Drain cooked pasta; top with sauce. Season with black pepper and salt.

NUTRITION FACTS:
386 calories; protein 15.5g; carbohydrates 57.9g; fat 10.3g;

Crispy Farro Cakes

Prep:
15 mins
Cook:
53 mins
Additional:
1 hr 10 mins
Total:
2 hrs 18 mins
Servings:
6
Yield:
6 servings

INGREDIENTS:

3 cloves garlic, minced
¼ cup finely diced red bell pepper
½ teaspoon freshly ground black pepper
1 ounce freshly grated Parmigiano-Reggiano cheese
1 large egg
1 pinch cayenne pepper
¼ cup olive oil for frying
3 cups water
1 cup farro, not rinsed
1 tablespoon kosher salt
2 sprigs fresh thyme
½ cup finely diced onion

DIRECTIONS:

1

Place water, farro, and salt in a large pot. Stir in thyme, onion, and garlic. Bring to a boil over high heat. Reduce heat to low, cover, and simmer until farro is very tender, 40 to 45 minutes. Drain well for about 10 minutes (do not rinse). Remove sprigs of thyme.

2

Transfer farro to a large bowl. While farro is still hot, add bell pepper, black pepper, grated cheese, egg, and cayenne pepper. Mix thoroughly; lightly tamp down. Allow mixture to come to room temperature. Cover with plastic wrap; refrigerate until thoroughly chilled, about 1 hour.

3

Heat oil in skillet over medium-high heat. Pack an ice cream scoop with farro mixture and turn out onto hot skillet. (Because there are no binders like flour or breadcrumbs, the cakes are almost impossible to form with your hands.) Gently press down farro cakes to slightly flatten them. After a minute or so when cakes are frying nicely, reduce heat to medium. Continue cooking the first side until you can see the bottom turning brown and a thick crust forming, 4 to 5 minutes. Do not flip until a crisp brown crust has formed.

4

Flip cakes and continue frying over medium heat until second side forms a crispy crust, 4 or 5 minutes.

NUTRITION FACTS:

149 calories; protein 6.6g; carbohydrates 25.1g; fat 3.9g;

Coconut chia pudding

Prep:

10 mins

Additional:

20 mins

Total:

30 mins

Servings:

6

Yield:

6 servings

INGREDIENTS:

6 tablespoons unsweetened coconut milk

1 tablespoon agave nectar, or more to taste

½ teaspoon vanilla extract

¼ teaspoon ground cinnamon

1 pinch salt

½ cup diced fresh strawberries (Optional)

½ cup chia seeds

2 cups coconut milk

DIRECTIONS:

1

Place chia seeds in a bowl.

2

Whisk coconut milk, unsweetened coconut milk, agave nectar, vanilla extract, cinnamon, and salt together in a bowl; pour over chia seeds and stir well. Allow coconut milk-chia seed mixture to soak until thickened, at least 20 minutes, or cover bowl with plastic wrap and refrigerate overnight.

3

Stir pudding and top with strawberries.

NUTRITION FACTS:

243 calories; protein 3.5g; carbohydrates 10.8g; fat 22.4g;

Hazelnut French Toast

Prep:

15 mins

Cook:

15 mins

Total:

30 mins

Servings:

6

Yield:

6 servings

INGREDIENTS:

2 tablespoons butter, divided, or more as needed

12 pieces brioche (about 1 1/2-inch thick)

1 cup toasted hazelnuts, chopped

1 cup beaten eggs

1 cup half-and-half

2 tablespoons hazelnut liqueur

½ cup maple syrup, or to taste

DIRECTIONS:

1

Whisk eggs, half-and-half, and hazelnut liqueur together in a shallow bowl.

2

Melt 1 teaspoon butter in a large skillet, tilting the skillet to assure complete coverage.

3

Dip 2 slices brioche in the egg mixture, moistening both sides.

4

Cook brioche in the hot skillet until golden brown, 2 to 4 minutes per side. Repeat process until all bread is cooked.

5

Cut each slice of brioche into half on a bias. Sprinkle hazelnuts over the halves and top with maple syrup.

NUTRITION FACTS:

905 calories; protein 24.7g; carbohydrates 97g; fat 46.9g;

Yogurt and Granola

Prep:

5 mins

Total:

5 mins

Servings:

1

Yield:

1 serving

INGREDIENTS:

1 tablespoon light agave syrup

1 tablespoon flaxseed meal

1 pinch ground cinnamon, or to taste

1 (6 ounce) container fat-free plain yogurt

¼ cup granola

DIRECTIONS:

1

Stir yogurt, granola, agave syrup, flaxseed meal, and cinnamon together in a bowl.

NUTRITION FACTS:

344 calories; protein 15.6g; carbohydrates 48.1g; fat 10.6g;

Sweet Peach Crepe Filling

Prep:

10 mins

Cook:

15 mins

Additional:

12 hrs 20 mins

Total:

12 hrs 45 mins

Servings:

12

Yield:

12 servings

INGREDIENTS:

1 ½ teaspoons vanilla extract

1 teaspoon ground nutmeg

1 (21 ounce) can peach pie filling

1 tablespoon lemon juice (Optional)

2 cups ricotta cheese

1 cup confectioners' sugar

2 teaspoons ground cinnamon

DIRECTIONS:

1

Drain ricotta cheese in cheesecloth placed over a bowl, 12 to 24 hours.

2

Combine drained ricotta, confectioners' sugar, cinnamon, vanilla extract, and nutmeg in a large bowl. Refrigerate immediately.

3

Spread peach pie filling into the bottom of a nonstick pot and add lemon juice. Cook over medium-low heat, stirring with a heat-resistant rubber spatula, until steam or bubbles begin to form. Use the spatula to roll filling together into the middle of the pan, and spread again. Repeat this process until filling is the consistency of honey.

4

While filling is still hot, scrape into a container and allow to cool, 20 to 30 minutes.

5

Take the cream filling out of the refrigerator. Combine fruit mixture with cream in a separate bowl, 1 spoonful of each at a time, until the consistency is that of cake frosting. Refrigerate until ready to serve.

NUTRITION FACTS:

141 calories; protein 4.9g; carbohydrates 23.4g; fat 3.1g;

Oat Pudding with Mango and Coconut

Prep:

10 mins

Cook:

15 mins

Additional:

15 mins

Total:

40 mins

Servings:

2

Yield:

2 cups

INGREDIENTS:

½ cup cashew milk

½ banana, chilled

1 mango, diced

½ cup coconut flakes

2 teaspoons raw honey

4 cups water

1 cup steel cut oats

1 pinch salt

DIRECTIONS:

1

Bring lightly salted water to boil in a pot. Stir oats into boiling water and reduce heat to medium-low. Cook and stir until oats soften and water is absorbed, about 15 minutes. Remove from heat and allow to cool, about 15 minutes.

2

Blend oats, cashew milk, and banana in a blender until smooth.

3

Spoon oat mixture into 2 bowls; top each with diced mango, coconut flakes, and honey.

NUTRITION FACTS:

482 calories; protein 11.3g; carbohydrates 89.2g; fat 10.5g;

Apple Muffins

Prep:
30 mins
Cook:
30 mins
Additional:
30 mins
Total:
1 hr 30 mins
Servings:
12
Yield:
1 dozen muffins

INGREDIENTS:

¾ cup apple juice
⅓ cup vegetable oil
1 egg
1 teaspoon ground cinnamon
1 cup apples - peeled, cored and finely diced
2 cups all-purpose flour
½ cup white sugar
3 teaspoons baking powder
½ teaspoon salt

DIRECTIONS:

1

Heat oven to 400 degrees F (205 degrees C). Grease bottoms only of 12 muffin cups or line with baking cups.

2

In a medium bowl, combine flour, sugar, baking powder, cinnamon, and salt; mix well. In a small bowl, combine apple juice, oil, and egg; blend well. Add dry ingredients all at once; stir just until dry ingredients are moistened (batter will be lumpy.) Stir in chopped apples.

3

Fill cups 2/3 full. Bake for 18 to 22 minutes or until toothpick inserted in center comes out clean. Cool 1 minute before removing from pan. Serve warm.

NUTRITION FACTS:

182 calories; protein 2.7g; carbohydrates 28g; fat 6.8g;

Blueberry Almond Yogurt

Prep:
5 mins
Total:
5 mins
Servings:
1
Yield:
1 serving

INGREDIENTS:

1 cup fresh blueberries
¼ cup milk
3 tablespoons slivered almonds
1 teaspoon chia seeds
1 cup nonfat plain Greek yogurt

DIRECTIONS:

1

Blend almonds and chia seeds together in a blender. Add yogurt, blueberries, and milk; blend until smooth.

NUTRITION FACTS:

369 calories; protein 27.4g; carbohydrates 38g; fat 12.8g;

Vegan Muesli

Prep:

10 mins

Additional:

8 hrs

Total:

8 hrs 10 mins

Servings:

6

Yield:

6 servings

INGREDIENTS:

½ lemon, juiced

2 cups sliced strawberries

1 cup blueberries

2 tablespoons maple syrup, or to taste

2 cups rolled oats

1 ½ (14 ounce) cans coconut milk, or more to taste

3 tablespoons chia seeds

2 Granny Smith apples, peeled and grated

DIRECTIONS:

1

Mix oats, coconut milk, and chia seeds together in a bowl.

2

Toss apples and lemon juice together in a bowl until coated; fold into oat mixture. Stir strawberries, blueberries, and maple syrup into oat mixture. Refrigerate for 8 hours to overnight.

NUTRITION FACTS:

392 calories; protein 7.1g; carbohydrates 42.2g; fat 24.6g;

Quinoa Bowl

Prep:

15 mins

Cook:

30 mins

Additional:

15 mins

Total:

1 hr

Servings:

6

Yield:

6 servings

INGREDIENTS:

1 clove garlic, chopped

1 cup asparagus, or more to taste

4 cups water

2 cups quinoa

1 cup cashews

1 tablespoon extra-virgin olive oil, or as needed

3 sweet potatoes, cut into 1/2-inch pieces, or more to taste

salt to taste

1 large yellow onion, chopped

DIRECTIONS:

1

Heat olive oil in a skillet over medium-high heat. Add sweet potatoes and salt; stir to coat sweet potatoes with oil and saute until tender yet firm to the bite, about 10 minutes. Transfer sweet potatoes to a plate and season with more salt.

2

Saute onion and garlic in the same skillet until softened, 4 to 5 minutes.

3

Place a steamer insert into a saucepan and fill with water to just below the bottom of the steamer. Bring water to a boil. Add asparagus, cover, and steam until tender, about 4 minutes. Cut asparagus into 1/2-inch pieces.

4

Bring water and quinoa to a boil in a saucepan. Reduce heat to medium-low, cover, and simmer until quinoa is tender and water has been absorbed, 10 to 15 minutes.

5

Toss sweet potatoes, onion-garlic mixture, asparagus, and quinoa together in a bowl; cool to room temperature. Add cashews and top with more olive oil and salt.

NUTRITION FACTS:

473 calories; protein 14.1g; carbohydrates 70g; fat 16.4g;

Apple, Carrot, and Chia Muffins

Prep:

20 mins

Cook:

25 mins

Additional:

5 mins

Total:

50 mins

Servings:

16

Yield:

16 muffins

INGREDIENTS:

½ cup honey

½ cup brown sugar

1 egg

1 teaspoon vanilla extract

1 cup diced apple

1 cup shredded carrot

2 tablespoons chia seeds

1 ¾ cups all-purpose flour

½ cup whole wheat flour

1 teaspoon baking soda

½ teaspoon salt

1 cup buttermilk

½ cup melted butter

DIRECTIONS:

1

Preheat the oven to 350 degrees F (175 degrees C). Line 16 muffin cups with liners.

2

Combine all-purpose flour, whole wheat flour, baking soda, and salt in a bowl.

3

Beat buttermilk, melted butter, honey, brown sugar, egg, and vanilla extract in another bowl. Stir in flour mixture. Fold in apple, carrot, and chia seeds. Spoon batter into the prepared muffin cups.

4

Bake in the preheated oven until a toothpick inserted into the center of a muffin comes out clean, about 25 minutes.

5

Cool for 5 minutes before transferring to a wire rack.

NUTRITION FACTS:

197 calories; protein 3.2g; carbohydrates 31.9g; fat 6.8g;

Lemony Quinoa

Prep:

15 mins

Cook:

10 mins

Total:

25 mins

Servings:

6

Yield:

6 servings

INGREDIENTS:

¼ cup fresh lemon juice

2 stalks celery, chopped

¼ red onion, chopped

¼ teaspoon cayenne pepper

½ teaspoon ground cumin

1 bunch fresh parsley, chopped

¼ cup pine nuts

1 cup quinoa

2 cups water

sea salt to taste

DIRECTIONS:

1

Toast the pine nuts briefly in a dry skillet over medium heat. This will take about 5 minutes, and stir constantly as they will burn easily. Set aside to cool.

2

In a saucepan, combine the quinoa, water and salt. Bring to a boil, then reduce heat to medium and cook until quinoa is tender and water has been absorbed, about 10 minutes. Cool slightly, then fluff with a fork.

3

Transfer the quinoa to a serving bowl and stir in the pine nuts, lemon juice, celery, onion, cayenne pepper, cumin and parsley. Adjust salt and pepper if needed before serving.

NUTRITION FACTS:

147 calories; protein 5.9g; carbohydrates 21.4g; fat 4.8g;

Chocolate Banana Oatmeal Porridge

Prep:

10 mins

Cook:

5 mins

Total:

15 mins

Servings:

2

Yield:

2 cups

INGREDIENTS:

½ cup brown sugar

1 banana, mashed

¼ cup semisweet chocolate chips

2 cups boiling water

1 cup rolled oats

¼ teaspoon salt

DIRECTIONS:

1

In a saucepan, combine water, oats and salt. Simmer 5 minutes uncovered, stirring occasionally. Remove from heat, cover, and let stand 3 minutes. Stir in brown sugar, banana and chocolate chips.

NUTRITION FACTS:

516 calories; protein 6.9g; carbohydrates 108.1g; fat 9.1g;

Pear-Pecan Cheese Ball

Prep:
15 mins
Additional:
1 hr
Total:
1 hr 15 mins
Servings:
24
Yield:
24 servings

INGREDIENTS:

1 (8 ounce) package reduced-fat cream cheese, softened
1 ¼ cups shredded extra-sharp Cheddar cheese
1 medium firm ripe pear, finely chopped
1 scallion, white and green separated, finely chopped
½ teaspoon salt
¼ teaspoon ground pepper
Plastic Wrap
⅓ cup finely chopped toasted pecans

DIRECTIONS:

1

Stir cream cheese, Cheddar, pear, scallion white, salt, and pepper together in a medium bowl.

2

Coat a large piece of plastic wrap with cooking spray. Scoop the cheese mixture onto it. Using the plastic wrap to help you, form the cheese mixture into a ball, then completely wrap in plastic. Refrigerate for at least 1 hour and up to 2 days.

3

Just before serving, combine pecans and the reserved scallion greens in a shallow dish. Roll the cheese ball in the mixture, pressing to adhere.

NUTRITION FACTS:

69 calories; protein 2.9g; carbohydrates 1.7g; fat 5.8g;

Blackberry Crisp

Prep:

10 mins

Cook:

35 mins

Total:

45 mins

Servings:

8

Yield:

1 8-inch square pan

INGREDIENTS:

¾ cup all-purpose flour, divided

½ cup butter, softened

1 cup rolled oats

1 cup brown sugar

4 cups fresh blackberries

DIRECTIONS:

1

Preheat oven to 350 degrees F (175 degrees C).

2

Combine oats, brown sugar, and 1/2 cup flour in a bowl. Cut butter into oat mixture using a pastry blender until mixture is moistened and crumbly.

3

Spread blackberries into an 8-inch square baking dish and mix in the remaining 1/4 cup flour until berries are coated. Sprinkle crumb topping over berries.

4

Bake in the preheated oven until golden brown, 35 to 40 minutes.

NUTRITION FACTS:

318 calories; protein 3.7g; carbohydrates 49.7g; fat 12.6g;

CHAPTER 2: SOUP RECIPES

Chicken Noodle Soup with Egg Noodles

Prep:

30 mins

Cook:

45 mins

Total:

1 hr 15 mins

Servings:

8

Yield:

8 servings

INGRDIENTS:

1 (8 ounce) package dried egg noodles

½ cup finely chopped fresh parsley

1 tablespoon freshly squeezed lemon juice

salt and ground black pepper to taste

1 (3 1/2) pound chicken, cut into 8 pieces

4 (16 ounce) cans low-sodium chicken broth

2 carrots, peeled and thinly sliced

2 stalks celery, sliced

½ cup chopped onion

DIRECTIONS:

1

Combine chicken and chicken broth in a large, heavy pot over medium-high heat; bring to a boil. Reduce heat, cover partially, and simmer until chicken is no longer pink at the bone and the juices run clear, about 20 minutes. An instant-read thermometer inserted near the bone should read 165 degrees F (74 degrees C). Remove chicken with tongs and transfer to a large bowl. Allow chicken and broth to cool slightly.

2

Remove skin and bones from cooled chicken and discard. Cut chicken meat into bite-sized pieces. Skim fat off the top of the cooled broth and discard.

3

Return chicken broth to a simmer. Add carrots, celery, and onion to the broth and simmer until vegetables soften, about 8 minutes. Stir in chicken, egg noodles, parsley, and lemon juice and simmer until noodles are tender, about 5 minutes. Season with salt and pepper.

NUTRITION FACTS:

335 calories; protein 25.7g; carbohydrates 24g; fat 14.6g;

Black Bean Vegetable Soup

Prep:

15 mins

Cook:

20 mins

Total:

35 mins

Servings:

8

Yield:

8 servings

INGREDIENTS:

4 cups chicken broth

3 (15 ounce) cans black beans, rinsed and drained, divided

1 (8.75 ounce) can whole kernel corn

¼ teaspoon ground black pepper

1 (14.5 ounce) can stewed tomatoes

1 tablespoon vegetable oil

4 carrots, chopped

1 onion, chopped

4 cloves garlic, minced

1 tablespoon chili powder

1 teaspoon ground cumin

DIRECTIONS:

1

Heat oil in a large saucepan over medium heat; cook and stir carrots, onion, and garlic until onion is softened, about 5 minutes. Stir chili powder and cumin into onion mixture; cook and stir until evenly coated, about 2 minutes.

2

Pour broth over onion mixture and add 1/2 of the black beans, corn, and black pepper. Bring broth mixture to a boil.

3

Blend tomatoes and remaining 1 1/2 cans black beans together in a food processor or blender until smooth; pour into broth mixture. Reduce heat to low, cover pot, and simmer until carrots are tender, 10 to 15 minutes.

NUTRITION FACTS:

232 calories; protein 12.1g; carbohydrates 41.7g; fat 3.1g;

Sweet Potato and Kale Soup

Prep:

20 mins

Cook:

25 mins

Total:

45 mins

Servings:

6

Yield:

6 servings

INGREDIENTS:

¾ teaspoon ground coriander

1 pound sweet potatoes, peeled and cut into 1/2-inch cubes

4 cups vegetable broth

4 cups chopped kale

1 (15.5 ounce) can chickpeas, drained

1 cup canned coconut milk

1 onion, diced

2 cloves garlic, minced

1 teaspoon ground turmeric

1 teaspoon salt

¾ teaspoon curry powder

DIRECTIONS:

1

Heat oil in a large stockpot over medium-high heat. Add onion and garlic and saute for 2 minutes. Stir in turmeric, coriander, curry powder, and coriander. Add sweet potatoes; saute for 2 to 3 minutes, stirring frequently.

2

Pour in broth and bring to a simmer. Cover and simmer until sweet potatoes have just begun to soften, 8 to 10 minutes. Stir in kale and chick peas; simmer for 5 minutes more. Stir in coconut milk and adjust salt to taste.

NUTRITION FACTS:

308 calories; protein 7.2g; carbohydrates 40.7g; fat 14g;

Vegan Kale and Chickpea Soup

Prep:
15 mins
Cook:
30 mins
Total:
45 mins
Servings:
4
Yield:
4 servings

INGREDIENTS:

4 cups chopped kale leaves
1 (15 ounce) can chickpeas (garbanzo beans), drained and rinsed
1 cube vegetable bouillon
¼ teaspoon curry powder
1 cup almond milk
cooking spray
1 teaspoon minced garlic
¼ cup minced onion
1 quart vegetable broth, divided

DIRECTIONS:

1

Spray the inside of a stockpot with cooking spray; place over medium heat. Cook and stir garlic in the stockpot until lightly browned, 2 to 3 minutes. Add onion and about 2 tablespoons vegetable broth to garlic; cook and stir until onion is translucent, 5 to 10 minutes.

2

Stir kale into onion mixture; cook until slightly wilted, 3 to 4 minutes. Add chickpeas, remaining vegetable broth, vegetable bouillon, and curry powder; bring to a boil. Reduce heat and simmer until heated through, about 15 minutes. Add almond milk and cook until heated through, 2 to 3 minutes.

NUTRITION FACTS:

169 calories; protein 7.1g; carbohydrates 31g; fat 2.5g;

Amazing Italian Three Bean Soup

Prep:

10 mins

Cook:

20 mins

Total:

30 mins

Servings:

8

Yield:

8 servings

INGREDIENTS:

1 (19 ounce) can garbanzo beans, undrained

1 (19 ounce) can lentils

3 tablespoons tomato paste

½ teaspoon dried oregano

½ teaspoon ground black pepper

1 teaspoon salt

4 ounces mozzarella cheese, shredded

1 tablespoon olive oil

2 onions, chopped

1 clove garlic, minced

1 (28 ounce) can diced tomatoes with juice

1 (19 ounce) can kidney beans, undrained

DIRECTIONS:

1

Heat a large pot over medium-high heat. Pour in oil and saute onion and garlic until golden-brown. Stir in tomatoes, kidney beans, garbanzo beans, lentils, tomato paste, oregano, pepper, and salt. Turn heat to low and simmer 20 minutes. Sprinkle in cheese and stir until melted. Serve immediately, or cool and freeze.

NUTRITION FACTS:

259 calories; protein 13.9g; carbohydrates 38.5g; fat 5.5g;

Brussels Sprouts and Barley Soup

Prep:
25 mins
Cook:
1 hr 10 mins
Total:
1 hr 35 mins
Servings:
12
Yield:
12 servings

INGREDIENTS:

⅓ cup barley
1 ½ pounds Brussels sprouts, trimmed and cut in half
½ cup chopped green bell pepper
1 teaspoon salt
½ teaspoon ground black pepper
¼ cup butter
½ cup all-purpose flour
12 cups chicken broth
1 cup chopped fresh green beans
1 ¼ cups cubed turnips
½ cup chopped leeks
½ cup chopped carrots

DIRECTIONS:

1

Measure the chicken broth into a large soup pot. Bring to a boil. Add the beans, turnips, leeks, carrots and barley; simmer over medium heat for 30 minutes. Add the Brussels sprouts and green pepper. Season with salt and pepper. Simmer until the sprouts are tender, about 30 minutes more.

2

Melt the butter in a small saucepan over medium heat, stirring until it starts to brown. Whisk in the flour until smooth. Stir this into the soup and simmer until thickened, about 10 minutes.

NUTRITION FACTS:

146 calories; protein 8.4g; carbohydrates 16.6g; fat 5.6g;

Spinach and White Bean Soup

Prep:

20 mins

Cook:

27 mins

Total:

47 mins

Servings:

2

Yield:

2 servings

INGREDIENTS:

2 cups chicken stock

1 (15 ounce) can white beans, drained

1 teaspoon dried oregano

½ teaspoon dried thyme

½ teaspoon salt

¼ teaspoon ground black pepper

2 tablespoons lemon juice

3 cups baby spinach

½ cup chopped carrot

3 tablespoons olive oil

1 shallot, finely chopped

3 cloves garlic, minced

DIRECTIONS:

1

Combine baby spinach and carrot in a food processor; pulse until finely chopped.

2

Heat oil in a large pot over medium heat. Cook and stir shallot and garlic in the hot oil until fragrant, 2 to 3 minutes. Stir in spinach and carrot mixture, chicken stock, white beans, oregano, thyme, salt, and pepper. Bring to a boil, stirring occasionally. Reduce heat and simmer until flavors combine, about 20 minutes.

3

Remove soup from heat and stir in lemon juice. Puree with an immersion blender until smooth.

NUTRITION FACTS:

488 calories; protein 18.7g; carbohydrates 58.7g; fat 21.9g;

Japanese Soup with Tofu and Mushrooms

Prep:
10 mins
Cook:
10 mins
Total:
20 mins
Servings:
2
Yield:
2 servings

INGREDIENTS:

1 tablespoon miso paste
1 tablespoon soy sauce
⅛ cup cubed soft tofu
1 green onion, chopped
3 cups prepared dashi stock
¼ cup sliced shiitake mushrooms

DIRECTIONS:

1

In a medium saucepan, bring stock to a boil; reduce heat to simmer, add mushrooms, and cook for 3 minutes. In a small bowl, mix miso paste and soy sauce together; stir into stock along with tofu. Simmer 5 minutes, and serve topped with with green onion.

NUTRITION FACTS:

100 calories; protein 11g; carbohydrates 4.8g; fat 3.9g;

Coconut Curry Butternut Squash Soup

Prep:
15 mins
Cook:
1 hr 33 mins
Additional:
15 mins
Total:
2 hrs 3 mins
Servings:
6
Yield:
6 servings

INGREDIENTS:

¼ teaspoon cayenne pepper
1 tablespoon butter
½ cup chopped yellow onion
1 teaspoon yellow curry powder
1 (13 ounce) can coconut milk
2 ½ cups vegetable stock, or more if needed
¼ teaspoon freshly grated nutmeg
½ cup pepitas (pumpkin seeds)
1 pinch freshly grated nutmeg, or to taste
1 butternut squash, halved and seeded
1 tablespoon butter, melted
1 teaspoon salt, divided
¾ teaspoon pumpkin pie spice, divided

DIRECTIONS:

1

Preheat oven to 425 degrees F (220 degrees C).

2

Place butternut squash in a baking dish, flesh side up. Brush 1 tablespoon melted butter over the flesh and top with 1/2 teaspoon salt, 1/2 teaspoon pumpkin pie spice, and cayenne pepper.

3

Roast in the preheated oven until tender, about 1 hour. Remove squash from oven and cool for 15 minutes.

4

Place a large stockpot over medium heat; add 1 tablespoon butter. Cook and stir onion in the melted butter for 2 minutes. Add curry powder; cook and stir for 1 minute. Stir in coconut milk; bring to a boil.

5

Scoop flesh from the butternut squash and add to coconut milk mixture; mix in remaining 1/2 teaspoon salt, 1/4 teaspoon pumpkin pie spice, vegetable stock, and 1/4 teaspoon nutmeg. Bring to a boil, reduce heat to low, and simmer until soup is heated through.

6

Blend soup using an immersion blender on low speed. Simmer until soup is smooth and thickened, about 20 minutes more. Add more vegetable stock for a thinner consistency and season with salt.

7

Ladle soup into bowls and top each with pepitas and a pinch of nutmeg.

NUTRITION FACTS:

315 calories; protein 6.5g; carbohydrates 27.6g; fat 22.8g;

Carrot Cream Soup with Ginger

Prep:
10 mins
Cook:
30 mins
Total:
40 mins
Servings:
4
Yield:
4 servings

INGREDIENTS:

2 ½ cups vegetable broth
1 teaspoon finely grated fresh ginger
salt and freshly ground black pepper to taste
1 pinch white sugar
1 tablespoon olive oil
2 onions, finely chopped
1 clove garlic, minced
3 cups peeled and chopped carrots
¾ cup heavy whipping cream

DIRECTIONS:

1

Heat oil in a large pot over medium-low heat and cook onions until soft and translucent, about 5 minutes. Add garlic and cook until fragrant, about 1 minute. Stir in carrots and cook until softened, 3 minutes more. Pour in vegetable broth and bring to a boil. Season with ginger, salt, pepper, and sugar. Cover, reduce heat, and simmer until vegetables are soft and cooked through, about 15 minutes.

2

Puree carrot soup with an immersion blender until smooth. Add heavy cream and heat through. Puree once more quickly with immersion blender, and season with salt and pepper.

NUTRITION FACTS:

292 calories; protein 3.8g; carbohydrates 25.2g; fat 20.6g;

Vegetarian Pasta e Fagioli

Servings:
6
Yield:
6 servings

INGREDIENTS:

16 ounces tomato sauce
salt and pepper to taste
1 pinch dried oregano
1 tablespoon white sugar
2 (15 ounce) cans cannellini beans
1 pound ditalini pasta
3 tablespoons olive oil
6 cloves garlic, chopped
1 onion, chopped
½ cup chopped mushrooms
1 medium head escarole - rinsed and quartered

DIRECTIONS:

1
Cook pasta in a large pot of boiling water until done, approximately 8 to 10 minutes. Drain pasta, but reserve water for later use.

2
In a large skillet over medium heat, warm oil and saute garlic, onion, and mushrooms until soft. Place escarole on top of vegetables in the skillet, and cover until the escarole is wilts. Stir in tomato sauce and beans. Season with oregano and sugar, and salt and pepper to taste. Simmer over low heat for approximately 15 to 20 minutes.

3

Mix the cooked pasta into the sauce. Mix in 1 cup of the reserved pasta water; stir in more if necessary to achieve desired consistency.

NUTRITION FACTS:

554 calories; protein 22.7g; carbohydrates 98.1g; fat 8.7g;

Fantastic Potato And Green Chile Soup

Prep:
15 mins
Cook:
50 mins
Total:
1 hr 5 mins
Servings:
8
Yield:
8 servings

INGREDIENTS:

2 cups milk
½ teaspoon ground cumin
½ teaspoon dried Mexican oregano
½ teaspoon salt, or to taste
1 cup shredded Monterey Jack cheese
1 cup shredded Cheddar cheese
ground black pepper to taste
4 tablespoons salted butter
1 medium onion, chopped
1 clove garlic, minced, or more to taste
4 medium potatoes, peeled and cubed, or more to taste
⅓ cup all purpose flour
2 cups beef broth
28 ounces canned roasted Hatch green chile peppers, diced

DIRECTIONS:

1

Heat butter in a large Dutch oven or heavy-bottomed soup pot over medium heat until melted. Add onion; cook and stir until translucent, about 5 minutes. Add garlic and cook until fragrant, about 1 minute. Stir in potatoes and cook for 1 minute.

2

Sprinkle in flour and stir until smooth. Cook for 1 minute, stirring continuously, until browned but not burned. Slowly pour in broth and stir until well incorporated; bring to a simmer. Cover and cook, stirring every 15 minutes, until potatoes are tender, about 30 minutes. Be sure the soup does not boil.

3

Stir in chile peppers, milk, cumin, oregano, and salt. Bring to a simmer, then immediately remove from heat; do not allow to boil. Add Monterey Jack cheese and Cheddar cheese; stir until melted. Season with pepper and serve.

NUTRITION FACTS:

343 calories; protein 14.9g; carbohydrates 36.2g; fat 16.3g;

Sunday Lunch Soup

Prep:

45 mins

Cook:

1 hr

Total:

1 hr 45 mins

Servings:

8

Yield:

8 servings

INGREDIENTS:

8 mushrooms, sliced

1 (10.75 ounce) can tomato puree

1 (11 ounce) can sweet corn, drained

¼ medium head cabbage, finely chopped

2 carrots, chopped

2 stalks celery, chopped

2 cubes chicken bouillon

2 tablespoons mixed spice

1 ¼ cups heavy cream

paprika, for garnish

2 skinless, boneless chicken breast halves

5 cups water

2 onions, chopped

2 cloves garlic, crushed

1 green chile pepper, seeded and diced

4 potatoes, chopped

1 zucchini, chopped

DIRECTIONS:

1

In a large saucepan, boil the chicken in 5 cups water for approximately 30 minutes. Drain, retaining liquid, and chop the chicken.

2

In the saucepan over medium heat, place approximately 2 tablespoons reserved liquid, onions, garlic and green chile pepper. Slowly cook and stir 5 minutes, or until tender. One at a time, while gradually adding the remaining liquid, mix in the chopped chicken, potatoes, zucchini, mushrooms, tomato puree, sweet corn, cabbage, carrots and celery. Pour in any remaining liquid, and stir in the chicken bouillon and mixed spice. Bring to a boil. Reduce heat and simmer 1 to 2 hours, stirring occasionally.

3

Before serving, stir in the heavy cream, mixing thoroughly. Serve with a sprinkling of paprika.

NUTRITION FACTS:

326 calories; protein 13.1g; carbohydrates 38.2g; fat 14.9g;

Roasted Pumpkin Soup with Apple and Ginger

Prep:

10 mins

Cook:

1 hr 15 mins

Total:

1 hr 25 mins

Servings:

4

Yield:

4 servings

INGREDIENTS:

1 apple, peeled and cut into cubes

3 cups chicken broth, or more as needed

1 tablespoon maple syrup

ground white pepper to taste

salt to taste

¾ cup water, or to taste

½ cup heavy cream (Optional)

2 (1 pound) sugar pumpkins, halved and seeded

1 tablespoon olive oil, or more as needed

2 tablespoons butter

1 small onion, chopped

1 (1/2 inch) piece fresh ginger, peeled and minced

DIRECTIONS:

1
Preheat the oven to 350 degrees F (175 degrees C). Line a baking sheet with parchment paper.

2
Brush pumpkin flesh with olive oil. Place pumpkins face down on the prepared baking sheet.

3
Bake in the preheated oven until pumpkins are easily pierced with a fork, 45 to 60 minutes. Remove from the oven, let cool for 10 minutes, and peel away skin. Set pumpkins aside.

4
Melt butter in a large pot over low heat. Add onion and ginger and cook until soft and translucent, about 10 minutes. Add apple and cook for 3 to 5 minutes. Pour in chicken broth and mix in pumpkins. Bring to a boil, reduce heat, and simmer until apple is soft, 10 to 15 minutes.

5
Puree soup using an immersion blender. Season with maple syrup, white pepper, and salt.

6
Add water and cream and heat until soup is hot, but not boiling. Taste and adjust seasoning.

NUTRITION FACTS:

244 calories; protein 3.9g; carbohydrates 26.1g; fat 15.4g;

Vegan Sweet Potato Soup with Kale Pesto

Prep:
30 mins
Cook:
10 mins
Total:
40 mins
Servings:
6
Yield:
6 servings

INGREDIENTS:

Soup:
2 tablespoons extra-virgin olive oil
½ cup chopped celery
⅔ cup chopped onion
¼ teaspoon cayenne pepper
¼ teaspoon ground cumin
salt and ground black pepper to taste
2 cups cooked and mashed sweet potatoes
1 cup canned unsweetened coconut milk
2 cloves garlic, minced
2 cups vegetable broth, or more to taste
¾ teaspoon ground turmeric
¾ teaspoon ground ginger

Pesto:

1 cup kale, stemmed and chopped

½ cup English walnuts, coarsely chopped

¼ cup nutritional yeast

½ lemon, juiced, or more to taste

1 clove garlic

salt and ground black pepper to taste

5 tablespoons extra-virgin olive oil, or more to taste

DIRECTIONS:

1

Heat olive oil in a large saucepan over medium heat until shimmering. Add celery and onion; cook and stir until the vegetables soften, 3 to 4 minutes. Stir in garlic and cook until fragrant, about 1 minute. Mix in broth, turmeric, ginger, cayenne, cumin, salt, and pepper. Bring to a boil.

2

Pour carefully into a high-speed blender, cover with a lid, and puree on high speed for 1 minute. Add mashed sweet potato and coconut milk; puree until soup has a creamy consistency, about 4 minutes. Add more broth or water if soup is too thick. Cover and keep warm.

3

Combine kale, walnuts, nutritional yeast, lemon juice, garlic, salt, and pepper in a blender or food processor. Process or blend at high speed into a paste, stopping to scrape down the sides of the bowl with a spatula as needed, about 3 minutes. Pour in olive oil, one tablespoon at a time, blending after each addition. Add more oil or lemon juice if pesto seems too thick.

4

Ladle the warm soup into bowls and spoon some pesto on top of each serving.

NUTRITION FACTS:

386 calories; protein 7.3g; carbohydrates 23.9g; fat 31g

Green Soup

Prep:
20 mins
Cook:
1 hr 20 mins
Total:
1 hr 40 mins
Servings:
8
Yield:
8 servings

INGREDIENTS:

1 pound fresh kale, chopped
12 ounces fresh spinach, chopped
2 ounces goat cheese, crumbled
1 tablespoon lemon juice
salt and ground black pepper to taste
1 tablespoon olive oil
2 large onions, chopped
8 cups vegetable broth
½ cup uncooked long-grain wild rice
4 cloves garlic, minced

DIRECTIONS:

1

Heat olive oil in a small frying pan over medium-high heat. Cook and stir onions in the hot oil until until translucent, about 5 minutes. Reduce heat to low and continue cooking and stirring until onion is very tender and dark brown, about 30 minutes more.

2

Pour vegetable broth into a pot and place over medium heat. Add rice and minced garlic; stir in kale and spinach, adding more broth if necessary. Add onions to the pot. Allow the greens to reduce and rice to fully cook, about 45 minutes.

3

Use an immersion blender to blend to desired consistency. Add goat cheese and use the blender again to create a creamy texture. Stir in lemon juice, salt, and pepper.

NUTRITION FACTS:

162 calories; protein 7.6g; carbohydrates 24g; fat 5g;

Easy Hot Bean Soup

Prep:
1 min
Cook:
5 mins
Total:
6 mins
Servings:
4
Yield:
4 servings

INGREDIENTS:

2 cups water
1 teaspoon chicken bouillon powder
1 cup pinto beans, drained
2 cups garbanzo beans, drained
¼ teaspoon hot pepper sauce

DIRECTIONS:

1
Place pinto beans and garbanzo beans in a medium sized stock pot with water. Cook for 5 minutes over medium-high heat and then add chicken bouillon granules. Mix well and add hot pepper sauce.

2
Once heated through mash the beans and serve.

NUTRITION FACTS:

197 calories; protein 9.1g; carbohydrates 36.5g; fat 2g;

Smoky Black Bean Soup

Prep:

20 mins

Cook:

55 mins

Total:

1 hr 15 mins

Servings:

10

Yield:

10 servings

INGREDIENTS:

1 green bell pepper, chopped

1 red bell pepper, chopped

3 cloves garlic, minced

1 chipotle chile in adobo sauce, finely chopped

2 teaspoons ground cumin

4 (15 ounce) cans black beans, rinsed and drained

4 cups chicken broth

1 tablespoon olive oil

4 ounces turkey bacon, finely chopped

1 onion, chopped

DIRECTIONS:

1

Heat olive oil in a large pot over medium heat. Cook and stir bacon, onion, green bell pepper, and red bell pepper in hot oil until the onion is caramelized, about 20 minutes.

2

Stir garlic, chipotle pepper, and cumin into the bacon mixture; cook until the garlic is fragrant, 1 to 2 minutes. Pour black beans and chicken broth into the pot; bring to a boil, reduce heat to medium-low, and simmer until the beans are tender, about 30 minutes.

3

Mash some of the beans with a potato masher until the soup reaches your desired consistency.

NUTRITION FACTS:

196 calories; protein 11.7g; carbohydrates 31.5g; fat 3g;

Vegan Mushroom and Kale Soup

Prep:

20 mins

Cook:

30 mins

Total:

50 mins

Servings:

4

Yield:

6 cups

INGREDIENTS:

1 ½ (32 fluid ounce) containers vegetable broth

2 (8 ounce) packages sliced mushrooms, divided

2 teaspoons salt

2 teaspoons herbes de Provence

1 teaspoon ground black pepper

1 bay leaf

2 cups chopped kale

1 tablespoon olive oil, or more to taste

2 russet potatoes, diced

2 carrots, diced, or more to taste

3 stalks celery, diced

1 onion, diced

DIRECTIONS:

1

Heat olive oil in a large saucepan over medium heat. Add potatoes, carrots, celery, and onion. Cook and stir until fragrant, 3 to 5 minutes. Add broth, 1 package of mushrooms, salt, herbes de Provence, pepper, and bay leaf. Cook until vegetables are soft, 15 to 20 minutes.

2

Place kale in a separate saucepan over low heat and add water to cover. Cook until tender, 5 to 8 minutes. Drain excess liquid.

3

Coarsely chop the second package of mushrooms.

4

Fill blender halfway with the vegetables and broth. Cover and hold lid down with a potholder; pulse a few times before leaving on to blend. Pour into a pot. Repeat with remaining vegetables and broth. Pour all of the pureed soup back into the saucepan. Add the kale and chopped mushrooms. Let simmer until mushrooms are just tender, 5 to 10 minutes more.

NUTRITION FACTS:

230 calories; protein 9.1g; carbohydrates 40.4g; fat 5g;

Broccoli Soup

Prep:
15 mins
Cook:
25 mins
Total:
40 mins
Servings:
8
Yield:
8 Servings

INGREDIENTS:

1 potato, peeled and chopped
4 cups chicken broth
¼ teaspoon ground nutmeg
1 tablespoon olive oil
1 large onion, chopped
3 cloves garlic, peeled and chopped
2 (10 ounce) packages chopped frozen broccoli, thawed
salt and pepper to taste

DIRECTIONS:

1

Heat olive oil in a large saucepan, and saute onion and garlic until tender. Mix in broccoli, potato, and chicken broth. Bring to a boil, reduce heat, and simmer 15 minutes, until vegetables are tender.

2

With a hand mixer or in a blender, puree the mixture until smooth. Return to the saucepan, and reheat. Season with nutmeg, salt, and pepper.

NUTRITION FACTS:

64 calories; protein 2.8g; carbohydrates 10.2g; fat 2g;

CHAPTER 3: SALAD RECIPES

Mediterranean Pasta Salad

Prep:
10 mins
Cook:
15 mins
Total:
25 mins
Servings:
2
Yield:
2 servings

INGREDIENTS:

1 tablespoon olive oil
1 tablespoon minced garlic
1 teaspoon lemon juice
salt and pepper to taste
1 cup macaroni
2 ounces roasted red bell peppers, diced
¼ cup sliced black olives
¼ cup crumbled feta cheese

DIRECTIONS:

1

In a small bowl or cup, combine olive oil and chopped garlic. Set aside.

2

Cook pasta in a large pot of boiling water until al dente. Drain.

3

Transfer pasta to a medium mixing bowl, and add roasted red peppers, olives, and feta cheese. Toss with olive oil mixture and lemon juice. Season with salt and pepper. Serve immediately.

NUTRITION FACTS:

340 calories; protein 10.3g; carbohydrates 44.2g; fat 13.6g;

Baby Bell Peppers with Chicken Salad

Prep:
20 mins
Total:
20 mins
Servings:
1
Yield:
1 serving

INGREDIENTS:

2 tablespoons light mayonnaise
3 baby bell peppers, halved and seeded
1 cup low-fat cottage cheese
1 cup fresh cherries
1 (12.5 fl oz) can chunk chicken breast, drained and flaked
1 small jalapeno pepper, diced
3 green onions, thinly sliced, divided

DIRECTIONS:

1

Mix chicken, jalapeno pepper, 2 green onions, and mayonnaise
together in bowl until thoroughly combined. Stuff each baby bell
pepper half with chicken mixture.

2

Mix half of the remaining green onion with cottage cheese; use the
other half to garnish stuffed baby bell peppers. Serve baby bell
peppers alongside cottage cheese mixture and cherries.

NUTRITION FACTS:

1101 calories; protein 110.4g; carbohydrates 53.2g; fat 50.1g;

Tasty Veggie Bulgur Salad

Prep:
15 mins
Cook:
5 mins
Additional:
20 mins
Total:
40 mins
Servings:
6
Yield:
6 servings

INGREDIENTS:

1 red bell pepper, finely chopped
7 green onions, finely chopped
½ cup minced fresh parsley
½ cup minced fresh mint leaves
1 teaspoon red pepper flakes, or to taste
2 tablespoons olive oil
juice of 1 fresh lemon
2 tablespoons pomegranate molasses
1 cup fine bulgur
1 cup boiling water
2 tablespoons olive oil
1 onion, finely chopped
2 large tomatoes, finely chopped
1 cucumber, diced
2 green bell peppers, finely chopped

DIRECTIONS:

1

Place the bulgur in a bowl; stir in the boiling water. Cover and let stand for 20 minutes.

2

Meanwhile, heat 2 tablespoons olive oil in a skillet over medium heat. Stir in the chopped onion; cook and stir until the onion has softened and turned translucent, about 5 minutes.

3

Drain the bulgur and return it to the bowl. Add the cooked onion, chopped tomatoes, cucumber, green and red bell peppers, green onions, parsley, mint, and red pepper flakes. Drizzle with 2 tablespoons olive oil, the lemon juice, and the pomegranate molasses. Toss gently until the salad is thoroughly combined. Serve immediately, or refrigerate until serving.

NUTRITION FACTS:

216 calories; protein 5.3g; carbohydrates 30.4g; fat 9.8g;

Watermelon, Feta and Cashew Salad

Prep:
15 mins
Total:
15 mins
Servings:
8
Yield:
8 servings

INGREDIENTS:

½ cup toasted cashews
¼ cup rice vinegar
¼ cup olive oil
salt and pepper to taste
2 tablespoons Fresh mint or basil leaves
1 small ripe seedless watermelon
1 head Bibb or Boston lettuce
4 ounces feta cheese

DIRECTIONS:

1

Halve watermelon; scoop out balls of melon with a melon baller into a bowl. Separate leaves of lettuce and arrange like cups in a layer on a serving platter. Place melon balls on the lettuce. Crumble feta cheese over the salad and top with toasted cashews.

2

Whisk rice vinegar, olive oil, salt and pepper together. Drizzle over the salad. Garnish with mint or basil leaves

NUTRITION FACTS:

200 calories; protein 4.7g; carbohydrates 16.7g; fat 14g;

Spinach, Tomato, and Feta Quinoa Salad

Prep:
10 mins
Cook:
15 mins
Additional:
35 mins
Total:
1 hr
Servings:
4
Yield:
4 servings

INGREDIENTS:

Salad:

2 cups water
1 teaspoon chicken bouillon granules
1 cup multi-colored quinoa
2 cups roughly chopped spinach

Dressing:

3 tablespoons almond oil
2 tablespoons extra-virgin olive oil
2 tablespoons champagne vinegar
1 teaspoon dried thyme
1 teaspoon dried basil
1 teaspoon minced garlic
¼ teaspoon kosher salt

Salad Ingredients:

3 on-the-vine tomatoes, diced
½ cup crumbled feta cheese, divided
freshly ground black pepper to taste

DIRECTIONS:

1

Bring water and bouillon to a boil in a saucepan. Add quinoa, reduce heat to low, cover, and cook until water is absorbed, about 15 minutes. Transfer quinoa to a bowl and cool slightly, 5 to 10 minutes. Stir spinach into quinoa and refrigerate until completely cooled, at least 30 minutes.

2

Whisk almond oil, olive oil, vinegar, thyme, basil, garlic, and salt together in a bowl until dressing is smooth.

3

Stir tomatoes, 1/2 of the feta cheese, and dressing into cooled quinoa until evenly coated; top with remaining feta cheese and ground black pepper.

NUTRITION FACTS:

388 calories; protein 10.3g; carbohydrates 34.6g; fat 23.9g;

Minty Green Bean Salad

Prep:
20 mins
Cook:
10 mins
Total:
30 mins
Servings:
4
Yield:
4 servings

INGREDIENTS:

3 tablespoons olive oil
1 tablespoon cider vinegar
½ tablespoon minced garlic
¼ teaspoon dried basil
¼ teaspoon prepared mustard
salt and pepper to taste
¼ cup water
1 teaspoon white sugar
1 pound fresh green beans
4 cloves garlic, thinly sliced
2 slices onion, chopped
1 sprig fresh mint leaves

DIRECTIONS:

1

In a medium saucepan, bring the water and sugar to a boil, and cook the green beans 10 minutes, or until tender but crisp; drain.

2

Transfer green beans to a medium bowl, and mix with garlic, onion, and mint.

3

In a small container with a lid, mix olive oil, cider vinegar, garlic, basil, mustard, salt, and pepper. Shake until well blended. Toss into the green bean mixture.

NUTRITION FACTS:

144 calories; protein 2.6g; carbohydrates 12.3g; fat 10.3g;

Potato and Mustard Greens Salad

Prep:
15 mins
Cook:
15 mins
Additional:
1 hr
Total:
1 hr 30 mins
Servings:
6
Yield:
6 servings

INGREDIENTS:

¼ cup olive oil
1 teaspoon sambal oelek (Thai chile paste) or plain hot sauce
salt and freshly ground black pepper to taste
½ cup chopped cornichons
1 cup washed and cut mustard greens
2 ½ pounds Yukon Gold potatoes, peeled and halved
4 cloves garlic, peeled and sliced
½ cup mayonnaise
⅓ cup white wine vinegar

DIRECTIONS:

1

Boil potatoes and garlic in a large pot of salted water until just tender, 15 to 20 minutes. Drain and let cool to room temperature. Discard the garlic.

2

Whisk mayonnaise, vinegar, olive oil, and sambal oelek together in a large bowl. Season with salt and pepper to taste.

3

Roughly chop cooled potatoes into a large bowl. Add cornichons, mustard greens, and mayonnaise mixture. Toss to coat. Cover and set aside in the refrigerator for 1 hour. Season with salt and pepper to taste.

NUTRITION FACTS:

370 calories; protein 4.6g; carbohydrates 36.7g; fat 23.8g;

Red Potato, Asparagus, and Artichoke Salad

Prep:
25 mins
Cook:
35 mins
Additional:
1 hr
Total:
2 hrs
Servings:
8
Yield:
8 servings

INGREDIENTS:

¼ cup fresh lemon juice
¾ cup olive oil
salt and ground black pepper to taste
¼ teaspoon cayenne pepper, or to taste
18 small red potatoes
3 pounds fresh asparagus, trimmed
2 (14 ounce) cans artichoke hearts, drained and quartered
3 tablespoons Dijon mustard
5 tablespoons minced fresh chives

DIRECTIONS:

1

Place the potatoes into a large pot and cover with salted water. Bring to a boil over high heat, then reduce heat to medium-low, cover, and simmer until tender, about 20 minutes. Drain and allow to steam dry for a minute or two. Allow to cool completely before cutting into bite-size cubes. Transfer to a large bowl

2

Bring a large pot of salted water to a boil over high heat. Add the asparagus spears, and cook until tender, about 3 minutes depending on size. Drain and immediately plunge into cold water to stop cooking. Cut the asparagus spears into 1 inch pieces. Place in the bowl with the potatoes. Stir in the artichokes, breaking them apart slightly as you put them in the bowl.

3

Combine the mustard and lemon juice in a bowl; whisk the oil gradually into the mustard and lemon juice until smooth. Season with salt, pepper, and cayenne pepper to taste. Drizzle over the vegetables; toss to coat. Sprinkle with chives to serve.

NUTRITION FACTS:

553 calories; protein 12.4g; carbohydrates 84g; fat 21g;

Italian Lentil Salad

Prep:
10 mins
Cook:
35 mins
Additional:
30 mins
Total:
1 hr 15 mins
Servings:
4
Yield:
4 servings

INGREDIENTS:

4 ounces thinly sliced prosciutto
1 bunch fresh basil, leaves stripped from stems
¼ cup balsamic vinaigrette dressing, or as needed
4 cups water
1 ½ cups dried lentils, rinsed
4 ounces fresh mozzarella cheese, sliced

DIRECTIONS:

1

Bring water to a boil in a saucepan; add lentils. Cover and simmer until lentils are tender, about 35 minutes. Drain and and cool to room temperature.

2

Divide lentils among 4 salad plates; layer with mozzarella cheese slices, prosciutto, and fresh basil. Drizzle balsamic vinaigrette over each salad.

NUTRITION FACTS:

435 calories; protein 29.3g; carbohydrates 39.1g; fat 18.8g;

Vegan Mediterranean Quinoa Salad

Prep:
25 mins
Cook:
20 mins
Additional:
15 mins
Total:
1 hr
Servings:
6
Yield:
6 servings

INGREDIENTS:

2 tablespoons olive oil
2 tablespoons fresh lemon juice
2 tablespoons chopped fresh mint
2 tablespoons chopped fresh parsley
¼ teaspoon ground black pepper
¼ cup toasted sliced almonds (Optional)
2 cups water
1 cup quinoa
½ teaspoon salt, divided
½ cup cherry tomatoes, halved
1 baby cucumber, sliced
¼ cup chopped red onion
¼ cup halved Kalamata olives
4 small radishes, quartered

DIRECTIONS:

1

Bring water to a boil in a saucepan. Add quinoa and 1/4 teaspoon salt. Reduce heat to medium-low. Simmer, covered, until quinoa is just tender and liquid is absorbed, 12 to 14 minutes. Remove from heat, uncover, and let cool completely.

2

Stir together cooled quinoa, tomatoes, cucumber, onion, olives, radishes, oil, lemon juice, mint, parsley, pepper, and remaining 1/4 teaspoon salt in a large bowl. Serve immediately or chill up to 2 hours. Sprinkle with almonds (if using) before serving.

NUTRITION FACTS:

191 calories; protein 5.2g; carbohydrates 21.3g; fat 9.8g;

Potato Salad with Radishes

Prep:
15 mins
Cook:
25 mins
Additional:
45 mins
Total:
1 hr 25 mins
Servings:
4
Yield:
4 servings

INGREDIENTS:

1 ¾ pounds Yukon Gold potatoes
1 white onion, chopped
2 bunches radishes, sliced

Dressing:

4 tablespoons red wine vinegar
1 teaspoon Dijon mustard
salt and freshly ground black pepper
½ cup extra-virgin olive oil
2 tablespoons chopped fresh chives

DIRECTIONS:

1

Place potatoes in a large pot and cover with salted water; bring to a boil. Reduce heat to medium-low and simmer until tender, 20 to 25 minutes. Drain.

2

Cool potatoes until easily handled. Peel and slice into a large bowl. Cool completely, about 30 minutes. Add onion and radishes.

3

Whisk red wine vinegar, mustard, salt, and pepper in a bowl or cup. Drizzle in olive oil, while whisking, until well combined. Stir in chives. Drizzle over potato mixture and carefully mix in. Set aside for 15 minutes. Season with salt and pepper.

NUTRITION FACTS:

422 calories; protein 4.4g; carbohydrates 38.5g; fat 28.3g;

Amazing Drunken Grapefruit Salad

Prep:
15 mins
Total:
15 mins
Servings:
8
Yield:
8 servings

INGREDIENTS:

3 fluid ounces gin
8 leaves fresh mint, minced
8 whole mint leaves
8 cups refrigerated grapefruit, drained and juice reserved
¼ cup white sugar

DIRECTIONS:

1

Mix grapefruit, 1/2 cup reserved juice, and sugar in a bowl until sugar dissolves. Transfer grapefruit mixture to 8 serving cups; top each with about 1 teaspoon gin. Sprinkle minced mint over each cup. Garnish each cup with 1 mint leaf.

NUTRITION FACTS:

140 calories; protein 1.4g; carbohydrates 28.6g; fat 0.2g;

Ripe Olive Potato Salad

Prep:
25 mins
Cook:
15 mins
Total:
40 mins
Servings:
9
Yield:
8 to 10 servings

INGREDIENTS:

¾ teaspoon dried dill weed
¼ teaspoon ground black pepper
1 cup plain yogurt
2 teaspoons prepared mustard
1 teaspoon honey
¼ teaspoon garlic salt
3 pounds potatoes
1 ⅔ cups black olives
1 cup chopped celery
⅓ cup chopped green onions
1 ½ tablespoons white wine vinegar
2 tablespoons vegetable oil
1 ½ teaspoons salt

DIRECTIONS:

1

Bring a large pot of salted water to a boil. Add potatoes; cook until tender but still firm, about 15 minutes. Drain and transfer to a large bowl; cool, peel and dice.

2

Add olives, celery and onions to potatoes and gently mix.

3

Whisk together the vinegar, oil, salt, dill weed and pepper. Pour over potatoes and mix gently to coat. Refrigerate.

4

Whisk together yogurt, mustard, honey and garlic salt. Pour over potato mixture and stir gently but thoroughly. Chill and serve.

NUTRITION FACTS:

197 calories; protein 4.4g; carbohydrates 30.8g; fat 6.9g;

Kale Salad with Balsamic Dressing

Prep:
20 mins
Additional:
30 mins
Total:
50 mins
Servings:
6
Yield:
6 servings

INGREDIENTS:

¼ cup balsamic vinegar
1 teaspoon soy sauce
½ clove garlic, crushed
½ cup sunflower seeds
1 bunch fresh kale, stems removed and leaves thinly sliced
1 teaspoon olive oil
1 pinch salt
5 slices bacon
¼ cup olive oil

DIRECTIONS:

1

Place kale in a resealable plastic bag; add 1 teaspoon olive oil and salt. Mix thoroughly until leaves are coated. Seal bag and let sit for 30 minutes.

2

Place bacon in a large skillet and cook over medium-high heat, turning occasionally, until evenly browned, about 10 minutes. Drain bacon slices on paper towels; crumble into small pieces.

3

Whisk 1/4 cup olive oil, balsamic vinegar, soy sauce, and garlic together in a bowl until dressing is evenly mixed.

4

Transfer kale to a bowl; add dressing and toss to coat. Top salad with bacon and sunflower seeds.

NUTRITION FACTS:

243 calories; protein 7.9g; carbohydrates 11.7g; fat 19.7g;

Chinese Napa Cabbage Salad

Prep:
10 mins
Cook:
15 mins
Total:
25 mins
Servings:
6
Yield:
6 servings

INGREDIENTS:

6 green onions, chopped
¼ cup vegetable oil
¼ cup rice wine vinegar
1 tablespoon soy sauce
1 tablespoon sesame oil
⅛ cup white sugar
1 (3 ounce) package chicken flavored ramen noodles
¼ cup butter
½ cup sesame seeds, toasted
½ cup blanched slivered almonds
1 large head napa cabbage, shredded

DIRECTIONS:

1

Crush noodles, place them in a medium skillet and brown in butter over medium heat. Add almonds and sesame seeds. Stir often to prevent burning. Add seasoning mix from noodles and cool. Toss in a large bowl with cabbage and onions.

2

Prepare the dressing by whisking together the vegetable oil, rice vinegar, soy sauce, sesame oil and sugar. Pour over salad, toss and serve.

NUTRITION FACTS:

405 calories; protein 9.2g; carbohydrates 28.3g; fat 30.3g;

Lettuce, Avocado and Sunflower Seed Salad

Prep:

15 mins

Total:

15 mins

Servings:

4

Yield:

4 servings

INGREDIENTS:

1 clove garlic, minced

1 tablespoon mayonnaise

2 heads Bibb lettuce - rinsed, dried and torn

⅓ cup sunflower seeds

2 avocados - peeled, pitted and sliced

½ cup olive oil

1 ½ tablespoons red wine vinegar

1 ½ tablespoons balsamic vinegar

DIRECTIONS:

1

Whisk together the olive oil, red wine vinegar, balsamic vinegar, garlic and mayonnaise. Season with salt and pepper to taste.

2

In a salad bowl, combine the lettuce and sunflower seeds. Toss with enough dressing to coat. Top with sliced avocado and serve.

NUTRITION FACTS:

442 calories; protein 3.2g; carbohydrates 12.2g; fat 44.7g;

Mediterranean Zucchini and Chickpea Salad

Prep:

25 mins

Total:

25 mins

Servings:

6

Yield:

6 servings

INGREDIENTS:

⅓ cup olive oil

⅓ cup packed fresh basil leaves, roughly chopped

¼ cup white balsamic vinegar

1 tablespoon chopped fresh rosemary

1 tablespoon capers, drained and chopped

1 clove garlic, minced

½ teaspoon dried Greek oregano

1 pinch crushed red pepper flakes (Optional)

salt and ground black pepper to taste

2 cups diced zucchini

1 (15 ounce) can chickpeas, drained and rinsed

1 cup halved grape tomatoes

¾ cup chopped red bell pepper

½ cup chopped sweet onion

½ cup crumbled feta cheese

½ cup chopped Kalamata olives

DIRECTIONS:

1

Mix zucchini, chickpeas, tomatoes, red bell pepper, onion, feta, Kalamata olives, olive oil, basil, vinegar, rosemary, capers, garlic, oregano, red pepper flakes, salt, and black pepper together in a large bowl.

NUTRITION FACTS:

258 calories; protein 5.6g; carbohydrates 19g; fat 18.5g;

Amazing Jicama And Pineapple Salad In A Cilantro Vinaigrette

Prep:

30 mins

Additional:

30 mins

Total:

1 hr

Servings:

4

Yield:

4 servings

INGREDIENTS:

1 bunch fresh cilantro, minced

½ teaspoon salt

¼ teaspoon ground black pepper

¼ cup olive oil

½ fresh pineapple - peeled, cored, and cut into chunks

1 jicama, peeled and julienned

3 cups mixed baby greens

1 avocado - peeled, pitted and diced

2 serrano peppers, seeded and minced

2 tablespoons fresh lime juice

2 tablespoons rice vinegar

DIRECTIONS:

1

Whisk together the serrano pepper, lime juice, rice vinegar, cilantro, salt, and pepper in a large bowl. Slowly drizzle in the olive oil while continually whisking. Add the pineapple and jicama; toss to coat. Allow to sit 30 minutes to 1 hour.

2

Place the spring mix in a large salad bowl; scatter the avocado over the lettuce; top with the marinated pineapple and jicama, drizzling the remaining vinaigrette over the salad. Serve NOW!

NUTRITION FACTS:

360 calories; protein 4.1g; carbohydrates 43.8g; fat 21.4g;

Broccoli Mango Salad

Prep:
20 mins
Additional:
4 hrs
Total:
4 hrs 20 mins
Servings:
8
Yield:
8 servings

INGREDIENTS:

4 cups chopped broccoli
1 large mango, peeled and cubed
½ cup cashews
1 small red onion, cut into thin wedges
1 (11 ounce) can mandarin oranges, drained
½ cup reduced-fat ranch dressing
2 tablespoons orange juice
1 tablespoon prepared horseradish

DIRECTIONS:

Instructions Checklist

1

Combine ranch dressing, orange juice, and horseradish in a bowl; mix well and set aside.

2

Toss together the chopped broccoli, cubed mango, cashews, and wedged onion in a salad bowl. Pour the dressing over the broccoli mixture; toss to coat. Refrigerate at least 4 hours. Add the drained oranges to the salad just before serving.

NUTRITION FACTS:

148 calories; protein 3.3g; carbohydrates 18.9g; fat 7.7g;

Mom's Mashed Potato Salad

Prep:
20 mins
Cook:
20 mins
Additional:
1 hr
Total:
1 hr 40 mins
Servings:
8
Yield:
8 servings

INGREDIENTS:

½ cup diced celery
¼ cup chopped sweet pickles
salt and ground black pepper to taste
1 cup mayonnaise
⅓ cup sweet pickle juice
1 teaspoon prepared yellow mustard
6 Yukon Gold potatoes
1 small sweet onion, diced
3 hard-cooked eggs, chopped

DIRECTIONS:

1

Place potatoes into a large pot and cover with salted water; bring to a boil. Reduce heat to medium-low and simmer until tender, about 20 minutes. Drain and transfer potatoes to a large bowl.

2

Mash potatoes with a potato masher. Stir in onion, eggs, celery, pickles, salt, and black pepper. Mix mayonnaise, pickle juice, and mustard in a separate bowl; pour over potatoes and mix well. Cover and refrigerate at least 1 hour before serving.

NUTRITION FACTS:

309 calories; protein 4.7g; carbohydrates 19.7g; fat 24g;

CHAPTER 4: LUNCH &

DINNER RECIPES

Mexican Black Beans and Rice

Prep:

10 mins

Cook:

20 mins

Total:

30 mins

Servings:

4

Yield:

4 servings

INGREDIENTS:

2 teaspoons chopped fresh oregano

2 teaspoons chopped fresh cilantro

1 (15 ounce) can black beans, rinsed and drained

½ cup mild salsa

¼ cup water, or as needed

2 cups cooked white rice

salt to taste

2 tablespoons coconut oil

1 teaspoon chili powder

1 teaspoon garlic powder

1 teaspoon ground cumin

1 teaspoon ground coriander

2 stalks celery, chopped

1 tomato, chopped

½ cup frozen corn

DIRECTIONS:

1

Heat coconut oil in a large skillet over medium-low heat. Add chili powder, garlic powder, cumin, and coriander; fry until fragrant, about 30 seconds. Add celery, cook and stir until softened, 3 to 5 minutes.

2

Add tomato, frozen corn, oregano, and cilantro; stir to coat. Stir in black beans and salsa. Bring to a simmer and cook for 10 to 15 minutes, adding water as needed to keep the mixture saucy.

3

Remove from the heat and stir in cooked rice until coated. Season with salt.

NUTRITION FACTS:

304 calories; protein 10.5g; carbohydrates 49.7g; fat 8g;

Bok Choy with Vegetables and Garlic Sauce

Prep:
20 mins
Cook:
15 mins
Total:
35 mins
Servings:
4
Yield:
4 servings

INGREDIENTS:

2 carrots, chopped
4 cups sliced bok choy
1 teaspoon white sugar
salt to taste
2 teaspoons sesame oil
2 teaspoons peanut oil
10 cloves garlic, crushed
1 tablespoon minced fresh ginger root
¼ cup vegetable broth
¼ cup water
1 red bell pepper, cubed

DIRECTIONS:

1

Heat peanut oil in a large nonstick skillet over medium-low heat. Cook garlic and ginger until fragrant, about 1 minute. Add vegetable broth and water. Cover and cook until garlic and ginger are very soft, about 7 minutes. Stir in bell pepper and carrots and cook for 1 minute. Add bok choy and toss until well coated with liquid. Season with sugar and salt and cook until tender, about 4 minutes more. Drizzle with sesame oil.

NUTRITION FACTS:

79 calories; protein 1.9g; carbohydrates 7.4g; fat 5.1g;

Pasta with Fresh Tomatoes and Corn

Prep:

20 mins

Cook:

10 mins

Total:

30 mins

Servings:

3

Yield:

3 to 4 servings

INGREDIENTS:

½ cup chopped green onions

1 teaspoon dried basil

salt to taste

ground black pepper to taste

1 tablespoon grated Parmesan cheese

2 teaspoons chopped fresh basil (Optional)

8 ounces pasta

4 tablespoons olive oil

2 tablespoons red wine vinegar

½ cup whole corn kernels, cooked

4 tomatoes, chopped

DIRECTIONS:

1

In a large pot with boiling salted water cook pasta until al dente. Drain.

2

Meanwhile, in a large bowl whisk together the olive oil, red wine vinegar, and dried basil. Add salt and pepper to taste. Stir in the tomatoes, corn kernels, and scallions. Let sit for 5 to 10 minutes.

3

Toss pasta with tomato mixture. Sprinkle with grated parmesan cheese. Garnish with fresh basil, if desired.

NUTRITION FACTS:

440 calories; protein 11.8g; carbohydrates 53.8g; fat 20.9g;

Vegan Sweet Potato Chickpea Curry

Prep:
10 mins
Cook:
20 mins
Total:
30 mins
Servings:
6
Yield:
6 servings

INGREDIENTS:

1 (14 ounce) can coconut milk
1 sweet potato, cubed
1 tablespoon garam masala
1 teaspoon ground cumin
1 teaspoon ground turmeric
½ teaspoon salt
¼ teaspoon red chile flakes
3 tablespoons olive oil
1 onion, chopped
2 cloves garlic, minced
2 teaspoons minced fresh ginger root
1 (15 ounce) can chickpeas, drained
1 (14.5 ounce) can diced tomatoes
1 cup baby spinach

DIRECTIONS:

1

Heat oil in a skillet over medium heat and cook onion, garlic, and ginger until softened, about 5 minutes. Add chickpeas, tomatoes, coconut milk, and sweet potato. Bring to a boil, reduce heat to low and simmer until tender, about 15 minutes.

2

Season with garam masala, cumin, turmeric, chile flakes, and salt. Add spinach right before serving.

NUTRITION FACTS:

293 calories; protein 5.1g; carbohydrates 22.3g; fat 21.6g;

Jackfruit Vegan Tacos

Prep:
10 mins
Cook:
3 mins
Total:
13 mins
Servings:
4
Yield:
4 servings

INGREDIENTS:

2 tablespoons taco seasoning mix, or to taste
4 taco shells
2 (20 ounce) cans jackfruit in brine - drained, rinsed, and cut into bite-sized pieces
1 tablespoon vegetable oil
1 tablespoon water, or more as needed
½ cup salsa, or to taste

DIRECTIONS:

1

Heat oil in a small saucepan over medium heat. Add jackfruit; cook and stir for 2 to 3 minutes. Add 1 tablespoon water and taco seasoning; stir until well combined, about 1 minute. Add additional water 1 tablespoon at a time as needed.

2

Place a small amount of jackfruit in each taco shell; add 2 tablespoons salsa.

NUTRITION FACTS:

258 calories; protein 1.6g; carbohydrates 27.8g; fat 13.3g;

Fantastic Vegan Mapo Tofu

Prep:
20 mins
Cook:
5 mins
Total:
25 mins
Servings:
4
Yield:
4 servings

INGREDIENTS:

3 tablespoons fermented black beans, roughly chopped
2 green onions, white parts only, chopped
6 cloves garlic, minced
1 tablespoon fresh ginger, minced
1 teaspoon Sichuan peppercorns
2 tablespoons chili bean paste (doubanjiang)
1 (14 ounce) container silken tofu, cut into 1-inch cubes
1 tablespoon chile oil
1 tablespoon sesame oil
½ cup vegetable broth
1 tablespoon maple syrup
2 teaspoons reduced sodium soy sauce
1 teaspoon cornstarch
1 tablespoon peanut oil
1 cup shiitake mushrooms, sliced
3 tablespoons peanuts, chopped

DIRECTIONS:

1

Mix vegetable broth, maple syrup, soy sauce, and cornstarch in a bowl.

2

Heat peanut oil in a wok over medium-high heat. Add mushrooms, black beans, green onions, garlic, ginger, and Sichuan peppercorns. Saute until aromatic, about 1 minute. Add chili bean paste and the soy sauce mixture. Cook and stir until thick, 3 to 5 minutes. Add tofu; cook until heated through, about 1 minute more.

3

Transfer cooked tofu to a serving dish; drizzle chile oil and sesame oil on top. Top with chopped peanuts.

NUTRITION FACTS:

255 calories; protein 13g; carbohydrates 15.8g; fat 16.3g;

Mexican Pasta

Prep:

5 mins

Cook:

15 mins

Total:

20 mins

Servings:

4

Yield:

4 servings

INGREDIENTS:

1 (15 ounce) can black beans, drained

1 (14.5 ounce) can peeled and diced tomatoes

¼ cup salsa

¼ cup sliced black olives

1 ½ tablespoons taco seasoning mix

salt and pepper to taste

½ pound seashell pasta

2 tablespoons olive oil

2 onions, chopped

1 green bell pepper, chopped

½ cup sweet corn kernels

DIRECTIONS:

1

Bring a large pot of lightly salted water to a boil. Add pasta and cook for 8 to 10 minutes or until al dente; drain.

2

While pasta is cooking, heat olive oil over medium heat in a large skillet. Cook onions and pepper in oil until lightly browned, 10 minutes. Stir in corn and heat through. Stir in black beans, tomatoes, salsa, olives, taco seasoning and salt and pepper and cook until thoroughly heated, 5 minutes.

3

Toss sauce with cooked pasta and serve.

NUTRITION FACTS:

358 calories; protein 10.3g; carbohydrates 59.5g; fat 9.4g;

Mexican Rice and Beans

Prep:

10 mins

Cook:

25 mins

Additional:

5 mins

Total:

40 mins

Servings:

4

Yield:

4 servings

INGREDIENTS:

1 cup basmati rice

2 teaspoons paprika

1 teaspoon ground cumin

1 teaspoon dried oregano

salt and ground black pepper to taste

2 tablespoons tomato paste

2 cups vegetable broth

1 (14 ounce) can pinto beans, rinsed and drained

2 tablespoons olive oil

1 small onion, diced

1 small poblano pepper, diced

1 clove garlic, chopped

DIRECTIONS:

1

Heat olive oil over medium-high heat. Add onion, poblano pepper, and garlic; saute for 2 to 3 minutes. Add rice. Cook, stirring occasionally, until rice is completely coated in oil, about 2 minutes. Season with paprika, cumin, oregano, salt, and pepper.

2

Stir in tomato paste and cook for 1 to 2 minutes. Add vegetable broth and pinto beans. Bring to a boil; reduce heat to low. Cover and simmer until rice is tender, 15 to 20 minutes. Remove from heat, keep covered, and let stand for at least 5 minutes. Fluff with a fork.

NUTRITION FACTS:

348 calories; protein 9.8g; carbohydrates 59.2g; fat 8.8g;

Teriyaki Stir-Fry Zoodles

Prep:
10 mins
Cook:
12 mins
Total:
22 mins
Servings:
2
Yield:
2 servings

INGREDIENTS:

½ large green bell pepper, thinly sliced
¼ large yellow onion, thinly sliced
1 head baby bok choy, chopped
1 large zucchini, cut into long strands
1 teaspoon garlic powder
1 tablespoon olive oil
2 tablespoons coconut aminos teriyaki sauce, divided
1 large carrot, thinly sliced

DIRECTIONS:

1

Heat olive oil and 1 tablespoon teriyaki sauce in a large skillet over medium heat. Add carrot, bell pepper, and onion; cook and stir until onions are translucent, about 5 minutes. Stir in bok choy, zucchini, and garlic powder. Drizzle on remaining teriyaki sauce. Cook, stirring occasionally, until zucchini is tender, about 7 minutes.

NUTRITION FACTS:
165 calories; protein 6.5g; carbohydrates 21.5g; fat 7.7g;

Grilled Portobello Mushrooms

Prep:
10 mins
Cook:
10 mins
Additional:
1 hr
Total:
1 hr 20 mins
Servings:
3
Yield:
3 servings

INGREDIENTS:

3 tablespoons chopped onion
4 cloves garlic, minced
4 tablespoons balsamic vinegar
3 mushrooms portobello mushrooms
¼ cup canola oil

DIRECTIONS:

1

Clean mushrooms and remove stems, reserve for other use. Place caps on a plate with the gills up.

2

In a small bowl, combine the oil, onion, garlic and vinegar. Pour mixture evenly over the mushroom caps and let stand for 1 hour.

3

Grill over hot grill for 10 minutes. Serve immediately.

NUTRITION FACTS:

217 calories; protein 3.2g; carbohydrates 11g; fat 19g;

Quinoa Pilaf With Mushrooms

Prep:
15 mins
Cook:
35 mins
Additional:
10 mins
Total:
1 hr
Servings:
4
Yield:
4 servings

INGREDIENTS:

½ teaspoon fresh thyme leaves
1 bay leaf
1 ½ teaspoons kosher salt
freshly ground black pepper to taste
3 cups vegetable stock
1 tablespoon olive oil
1 small shallot, chopped
½ cup thinly sliced cremini mushrooms
1 ½ cups quinoa, rinsed and drained

DIRECTIONS:

1

Heat a large saucepan over medium heat and swirl olive oil around the inside of the pan to coat. Cook shallot in the hot oil until translucent, about 3 minutes; stir in cremini mushrooms, cooking and stirring until mushrooms are browned, 8 to 10 minutes. Stir quinoa, thyme, bay leaf, kosher salt, and black pepper into mushroom mixture. Cook, stirring often, until quinoa gives off a slightly toasted fragrance, about 5 minutes.

2

Pour vegetable stock into quinoa mixture (stock may spatter a bit); stir to combine. Bring to a full boil, reduce heat to low, and cover pan; simmer until liquid is absorbed, about 15 minutes. Remove from heat and fluff quinoa pilaf with a fork; cover pan and let pilaf stand 10 more minutes to steam dry.

NUTRITION FACTS:

290 calories; protein 9.9g; carbohydrates 45.4g; fat 7.4g;

Curry Tofu Stir-Fry

Prep:
10 mins
Cook:
25 mins
Total:
35 mins
Servings:
4
Yield:
4 main-dish servings

INGREDIENTS:

1 tablespoon chopped garlic
3 cups fresh spinach
2 tablespoons soy sauce
1 ½ tablespoons curry powder
1 teaspoon red pepper flakes (Optional)
cooking spray
1 pound extra-firm tofu, cut into 1-inch cubes
1 tablespoon vegetable oil
1 cup sliced fresh mushrooms

DIRECTIONS:

1

Preheat oven to 400 degrees F (200 degrees C). Spray a baking sheet with baking spray; arrange tofu in a single layer.

2

Bake tofu in preheated oven until evenly browned, flipping after 10 minutes, about 20 minutes total.

3

Heat vegetable oil in a wok or large skillet over medium-high heat. Add mushrooms and garlic; cook and stir until mushrooms are tender; 2 to 3 minutes. Add tofu, spinach, soy sauce, and curry powder; cook and stir until spinach is wilted; 3 to 5 minutes. Sprinkle red pepper flakes over mixture.

NUTRITION FACTS:

143 calories; protein 11.4g; carbohydrates 6.6g; fat 9.4g;

Tofu Stir-Fry with Peanut Sauce (Vegan)

Prep:
20 mins
Cook:
20 mins
Total:
40 mins
Servings:
4
Yield:
4 servings

INGREDIENTS:

½ teaspoon ground chile pepper

1 tablespoon olive oil

2 carrots, diced

1 red bell pepper, diced

1 (14 ounce) package firm tofu, drained and cut into 1-inch cubes

4 garlic cloves, minced

2 tablespoons minced fresh ginger

4 cups baby spinach

1 ½ cups cooked brown rice

1 (14 ounce) can light coconut milk

¼ cup peanut butter

2 tablespoons soy sauce

2 tablespoons brown sugar

1 tablespoon lime juice

1 teaspoon sriracha sauce

DIRECTIONS:

1

Whisk coconut milk, peanut butter, soy sauce, brown sugar, lime juice, sriracha sauce, and ground chile powder in a bowl until a smooth sauce forms.

2

Heat oil in a large skillet over medium-high heat. Add carrots and red bell pepper; saute until just tender, 1 to 2 minutes. Add tofu; saute until lightly browned, about 4 minutes per side. Add garlic and ginger; cook and stir until fragrant, about 30 seconds.

3

Pour sauce into the skillet; stir to coat tofu, carrots, and bell pepper. Cook until flavors combine, about 5 minutes. Reduce heat to low; stir in spinach 1 cup at a time until wilted. Serve over brown rice.

NUTRITION FACTS:

441 calories; protein 16.7g; carbohydrates 39g; fat 25.9g;

Garbanzo Stir-Fry

Prep:

15 mins

Cook:

30 mins

Total:

45 mins

Servings:

4

Yield:

4 servings

INGREDIENTS:

1 (15 ounce) can garbanzo beans, drained and rinsed

1 large zucchini, halved and sliced

½ cup sliced mushrooms

1 tablespoon chopped fresh cilantro

1 tomato, chopped

2 tablespoons olive oil

1 tablespoon chopped fresh oregano

1 tablespoon chopped fresh basil

1 clove garlic, crushed

ground black pepper to taste

DIRECTIONS:

1

Heat oil in a large skillet over medium heat. Stir in oregano, basil, garlic, and pepper. Add the garbanzo beans and zucchini, stirring well to coat with oil and herbs. Cook, covered, for 10 minutes, stirring occasionally.

2

Stir in mushrooms and cilantro, and cook until tender, stirring occasionally. Place the chopped tomato on top of the mixture. Cover, and let the tomatoes steam for a few minutes, but don't let them get mushy. Serve immediately.

NUTRITION FACTS:

167 calories; protein 4.6g; carbohydrates 21.2g; fat 7.7g;

Vegan Taco Chili

Prep:
10 mins
Cook:
1 hr
Total:
1 hr 10 mins
Servings:
10
Yield:
10 servings

INGREDIENTS:

1 (29 ounce) can tomato sauce
1 (6 ounce) can tomato paste
3 (15 ounce) cans kidney beans
1 (11 ounce) can Mexican-style corn
1 tablespoon olive oil
1 pound sliced fresh mushrooms
2 cloves garlic, minced
1 small onion, finely chopped
2 stalks celery, chopped

DIRECTIONS:

1

Heat the oil in a large skillet. Sautee the mushrooms, garlic, onion and celery until tender. Transfer them to a stock pot or slow cooker. Stir in the tomato sauce, tomato paste, beans and Mexican-style corn. Cook for at least an hour to blend the flavors.

NUTRITION FACTS:
190 calories; protein 10.9g; carbohydrates 35.1g; fat 2.4g;

Black-Eyed Peas and Tortillas

Prep:
10 mins
Cook:
15 mins
Total:
25 mins
Servings:
4
Yield:
4 servings

INGREDIENTS:

1 fresh jalapeno pepper, chopped
1 clove garlic, minced
1 tablespoon fresh lime juice
salt and pepper to taste
4 (12 inch) flour tortillas
1 tablespoon olive oil
¼ cup finely chopped onion
1 (15.5 ounce) can black-eyed peas, drained
½ cup vegetable stock

DIRECTIONS:

1

Heat the olive oil in a medium skillet over medium heat, and cook the onion until tender. Mix in the black-eyed peas, vegetable stock, jalapeno, garlic, and lime juice. Season with salt and pepper to taste, and continue cooking until heated through. Wrap the mixture in the tortillas to serve.

NUTRITION FACTS:

487 calories; protein 15.1g; carbohydrates 76.8g; fat 13.2g;

Tasty Vegan Eggplant Curry With Fresh Mint

Prep:

20 mins

Cook:

15 mins

Total:

35 mins

Servings:

2

Yield:

2 servings

INGREDIENTS:

2 red bell peppers, seeded and cut into strips

¼ teaspoon curry powder

1 cup coconut milk

salt and ground black pepper to taste

1 bunch fresh mint, minced

2 tablespoons vegetable oil

2 eggplants, cubed

1 bunch spring onions, minced

2 cloves garlic, minced

DIRECTIONS:

1

Line a plate with paper towels. Heat vegetable oil in a wok or large saucepan over high heat. Add eggplant; cook and stir until softened, 2 to 3 minutes. Remove eggplant from wok; drain on paper towels.

2

Combine onions and garlic in the same pan. Add red bell peppers; cook and stir for 3 minutes. Season with curry powder. Pour in coconut milk and season with salt and pepper. Bring to a simmer and add eggplant. Increase heat to high and bring to a boil. Cook, stirring constantly, until flavors are combined, about 3 minutes. Sprinkle with mint.

NUTRITION FACTS:

549 calories; protein 12g; carbohydrates 50.9g; fat 39.4g

Braised Fennel with Tomatoes and Feta

Prep:

15 mins

Cook:

20 mins

Total:

35 mins

Servings:

4

Yield:

4 servings

INGREDIENTS:

2 tablespoons chopped garlic

1 tablespoon lemon juice

¼ teaspoon salt

3 tablespoons crumbled feta cheese

2 bulbs fennel, cut into 8 wedges, fronds reserved

2 teaspoons ground coriander

2 tablespoons olive oil

1 ½ cups chopped tomatoes

DIRECTIONS:

1

Preheat the oven to 325 degrees F (165 degrees C). Sprinkle fennel wedges with coriander.

2

Heat oil in a large oven-proof skillet over medium-high heat. Add fennel; cook for 4 minutes. Flip. Add tomatoes, garlic, lemon juice, and salt.

3

Transfer skillet to the oven and bake for 15 minutes. Sprinkle with feta and fennel fronds.

NUTRITION FACTS:

138 calories; protein 3.5g; carbohydrates 13.7g; fat 8.8g;

Green Lentils and Rice Assyrian Style

Prep:
10 mins
Cook:
30 mins
Total:
40 mins
Servings:
8
Yield:
8 servings

INGREDIENTS:

4 tablespoons olive oil, divided
1 cup basmati rice
1 large onion, chopped
1 cup dry green lentils
2 cups water
¾ teaspoon salt, or to taste

DIRECTIONS:

1

Place the lentils into a pot and cover with the water. Bring to a rolling boil over high heat for 5 minutes, then cover and remove from heat. Meanwhile, rinse the rice in cold water until water comes out clear.

2

Heat 2 tablespoons olive oil or vegetable oil in a skillet over medium heat. Stir in the rice for about 1 minute, until the grains turn opaque and white, then stir in the lentils and water. Bring the rice mixture to a boil, then cover and reduce heat to medium-low for 5 minutes. Stir once, then cover and reduce heat further to low. Continue cooking, covered (don't remove the lid!) until the rice is tender, about 15 minutes more.

3

Meanwhile, heat the remaining 2 tablespoons of oil in the skillet over medium heat. Stir in the onion; cook and stir until the onion has softened and turned translucent, about 5 minutes. Reduce heat to medium-low, and continue cooking and stirring until the onion is very tender and dark brown, 15 to 20 minutes more. When the rice is ready, stir in the caramelized onion and season with salt.

NUTRITION FACTS:

235 calories; protein 8.2g; carbohydrates 34.6g; fat 7.3g;

Mushroom Kabobs

Prep:
30 mins
Cook:
10 mins
Total:
40 mins
Servings:
4
Yield:
4 servings

INGREDIENTS:

1 clove garlic, minced
2 teaspoons chopped fresh thyme
1 teaspoon chopped fresh rosemary
¼ teaspoon salt
¼ teaspoon ground black pepper
¾ cup sliced fresh mushrooms
2 red bell peppers, chopped
1 green bell pepper, cut into 1 inch pieces
¼ cup olive oil
2 tablespoons lemon juice

DIRECTIONS:

1

Preheat grill for medium heat.

2

Thread mushrooms and peppers alternately on skewers.

3

In a small bowl, mix together olive oil, lemon juice, garlic, thyme, rosemary, and salt and pepper. Brush mushrooms and peppers with this flavored oil.

4

Brush grate with oil, and place kabobs on the grill. Baste frequently with oil mixture. Cook for about 4 to 6 minutes, or until mushrooms are tender and thoroughly cooked.

NUTRITION FACTS:

151 calories; protein 1.4g; carbohydrates 6.5g; fat 13.8g;

Grilled Vegetables in Balsamic Tomato Sauce with Couscous

Prep:
20 mins
Cook:
15 mins
Total:
35 mins
Servings:
4
Yield:
4 servings

INGREDIENTS:

¾ cup frozen broad beans
1 (14.5 ounce) can diced tomatoes
2 tablespoons balsamic vinegar
1 cup couscous
1 cup vegetable stock
1 tablespoon olive oil
1 red bell pepper
1 zucchini
1 small eggplant
1 large sweet onion

DIRECTIONS:

1

Remove the seeds from the pepper, and chop into strips about 1 to 2 inches long. Cut the eggplant crossways into rounds about 1/3 to 1/2 inch thick, and cut each one into 6 to 8 even chunks. Peel the onion, and chop into 8 portions. Trim the zucchini, and cut into thick slices.

2

Heat grill pan over a high heat with a generous splash of olive oil. When it is very hot, add all the vegetables to the pan. Press down occasionally to get grill lines across them. Turn occasionally to prevent burning. Cook for about 15 minutes, or until the vegetables are evenly browned and cooked through.

3

Stir broad beans into the vegetables. Add chopped tomatoes, and vinegar. Simmer for a few minutes while the couscous is prepared.

4

Place couscous into a medium bowl. Add boiling vegetable stock, and stir with a fork. Keep lifting the couscous occasionally to prevent it sticking. It only takes 2 to 3 minutes to become soft. Place couscous in a large bowl or serving platter, and serve the vegetables on top.

NUTRITION FACTS:

317 calories; protein 10.7g; carbohydrates 59.2g; fat 4.5g;

Onion Spaghetti

Prep:
10 mins
Cook:
30 mins
Total:
40 mins
Servings:
6
Yield:
6 servings

INGREDIENTS:

1 (14.5 ounce) can whole peeled tomatoes
1 teaspoon salt
½ teaspoon freshly ground black pepper
1 tablespoon chopped fresh basil
¼ cup water
1 pound spaghetti
2 tablespoons olive oil
4 large onions, sliced
2 cloves garlic, crushed
1 tablespoon tomato paste

DIRECTIONS:

1

Heat oil in a large skillet over medium heat. Cook onions and garlic in oil until soft. Stir in tomato paste, tomatoes, salt, pepper, basil and water. Cover, reduce heat to low, and simmer 20 minutes, until thickened.

2

While sauce is simmering, bring a large pot of lightly salted water to a boil. Add pasta and cook for 8 to 10 minutes or until al dente; drain.

3

Toss sauce with hot pasta.

NUTRITION FACTS:

380 calories; protein 12g; carbohydrates 70.3g; fat 5.9g;

Peanut-Ginger Chickpea Curry

Prep:

5 mins

Cook:

25 mins

Total:

30 mins

Servings:

6

Yield:

6 servings

INGREDIENTS:

2 (14.5 ounce) cans chickpeas (garbanzo beans), rinsed and drained

2 teaspoons ground ginger, or to taste

⅛ teaspoon ground cinnamon, or to taste

⅛ teaspoon cayenne pepper, or to taste

1 (28 ounce) can diced tomatoes, drained

1 teaspoon salt

1 ½ cups white rice

3 cups water

1 (14 ounce) can coconut milk

5 tablespoons peanut butter

DIRECTIONS:

1

Bring the rice and water to a boil in a saucepan. Reduce heat to medium-low, cover, and simmer until the rice is tender and the liquid has been absorbed, 20 to 25 minutes.

2

Meanwhile, stir coconut milk and peanut butter together in a large saucepan over medium-high heat until the peanut butter melts and the mixture is smooth, 5 to 7 minutes. Stir chickpeas, ginger, cinnamon, and cayenne pepper into the mixture; cook, stirring occasionally, until the chickpeas are tender, about 10 minutes. Add tomatoes; continue cooking until the mixture thickens slightly, about 10 minutes. Season with salt. Serve with the rice.

NUTRITION FACTS:

581 calories; protein 16.4g; carbohydrates 79.3g; fat 22.8g;

Quinoa Almond Pilaf

Prep:
20 mins
Cook:
25 mins
Total:
45 mins
Servings:
3
Yield:
3 servings

INGREDIENTS:

1 clove garlic, minced
8 almonds, coarsely chopped
1 small tomato, seeded and chopped
2 tablespoons raisins
⅛ teaspoon salt
⅛ teaspoon ground black pepper
⅛ teaspoon dried thyme
⅛ teaspoon dried oregano
½ cup quinoa, rinsed and drained
1 cup cold water
¼ teaspoon salt
3 tablespoons olive oil
1 celery rib, chopped
1 small onion, chopped
1 carrot, chopped
1 pinch coarse sea salt

DIRECTIONS:

1

Combine quinoa, cold water, and salt in a saucepan; bring to a boil, reduce heat to medium-low, place a cover on the saucepan, and cook until the liquid is fully absorbed, about 15 minutes.

2

Heat olive oil in a skillet over medium heat. Cook and stir celery, onion, carrot, and garlic in the hot oil until the onion is translucent, 5 to 7 minutes. Stir almonds, tomato, raisins, salt, pepper, thyme, and oregano into the vegetable mixture; cook and stir 1 minute more.

3

Fluff the quinoa with a fork and stir into the mixture in the skillet; cook and stir until evenly mixed and hot, about 30 seconds.

4

Divide between 3 plates; sprinkle the top of each portion with a scattering of a few coarse sea salt granules for a surprising crunch of salty goodness.

NUTRITION FACTS:

303 calories; protein 6.2g; carbohydrates 33g; fat 17.1g;

Shiitake Scallopine

Prep:

10 mins

Cook:

20 mins

Total:

30 mins

Servings:

8

Yield:

8 servings

INGREDIENTS:

2 bulbs shallots, minced

1 pound shiitake mushrooms, thinly sliced

½ teaspoon dried thyme

½ cup white wine

4 (6 ounce) cans marinated artichoke hearts, drained and chopped

¼ cup small capers

1 pound angel hair pasta

¼ cup extra virgin olive oil

2 cloves garlic, minced

DIRECTIONS:

1

Bring a large pot of lightly salted water to a boil. Add pasta and cook for 8 to 10 minutes or until al dente; drain.

2

Heat oil in a large heavy skillet over low heat; sweat garlic and shallots until they start to become aromatic. Increase heat to medium and add mushrooms and thyme; saute until mushrooms begin to soften, about 3 minutes. Deglaze pan with wine and simmer 2 minutes. Stir in artichokes and capers and simmer 2 to 3 minutes more.

3

Pour mushroom mixture over pasta and serve.

NUTRITION FACTS:

354 calories; protein 10.4g; carbohydrates 51.2g; fat 13.2g;

White Chili

Prep:
15 mins
Cook:
30 mins
Total:
45 mins
Servings:
8
Yield:
8 servings

INGREDIENTS:

1 cup frozen corn kernels
1 cup water
2 (14 ounce) cans great Northern beans, rinsed and drained
12 ounces pepper jack cheese, cubed
1 pound ground turkey, browned
1 cup medium salsa

DIRECTIONS:

1

In a large pot or saucepan, combine the browned turkey, salsa, corn, water, beans and cheese. Stir together and simmer over low heat for about 30 minutes, or until cheese has melted and chili is hot.

NUTRITION FACTS:

390 calories; protein 28.8g; carbohydrates 28.4g; fat 18.6g;

Coconut Curry Chili

Prep:
10 mins
Cook:
1 hr 10 mins
Total:
1 hr 20 mins
Servings:
6
Yield:
6 servings

INGREDIENTS:

½ cup chopped carrot
¼ cup mango chutney
3 tablespoons curry powder
1 teaspoon onion powder
salt and ground black pepper to taste
½ cup coconut milk, divided
½ pound ground turkey
2 (10.75 ounce) cans tomato soup
1 ¼ cups water
1 tablespoon minced garlic
1 (15 ounce) can chickpeas (garbanzo beans), drained and rinsed
1 (15 ounce) can red kidney beans, drained and rinsed

DIRECTIONS:

1

Break the ground turkey into small pieces into a large skillet over medium heat. Cook and stir the turkey, continuing to break it into smaller pieces, until completely browned, 5 to 7 minutes. Drain as much grease as possible from the turkey.

2

Combine tomato soup, water, and minced garlic in a large pot; bring to a boil. Add the turkey to the pot and return the mixture to a boil and reduce heat to medium-low. Stir chickpeas, red kidney beans, carrot, chutney, curry powder, onion powder, salt, and black pepper through the turkey mixture; bring to a simmer, place a cover on the pot, and cook until the chickpeas are tender, about 15 minutes.

3

Stir 1/4 cup coconut milk through the chili, return cover to the pot, and simmer another 15 minutes. Pour the remaining 1/4 cup coconut milk into the chili, stir, and simmer 30 minutes more.

NUTRITION FACTS:

312 calories; protein 16.4g; carbohydrates 43.4g; fat 9.7g;

Vegetarian Collard Greens

Prep:
20 mins
Cook:
40 mins
Total:
1 hr
Servings:
6
Yield:
6 servings

INGREDIENTS:

2 (14 ounce) cans chopped tomatoes
1 cup vegetable broth
1 tablespoon brown sugar
1 tablespoon molasses
1 tablespoon liquid smoke flavoring
2 pounds collard greens, chopped
1 ½ cups cooked white beans (Optional)
1 tablespoon olive oil
1 tablespoon butter
1 large onion, halved and thinly sliced
4 cloves garlic, thinly sliced
2 sprigs fresh thyme, leaves stripped
2 bay leaves

DIRECTIONS:

1

Heat olive oil and butter in a large pot over medium heat until butter melts and starts to brown, 1 to 2 minutes. Add onion and garlic; cook and stir until onion turns translucent, about 5 minutes. Stir in thyme and bay leaves.

2

Pour chopped tomatoes, vegetable broth, brown sugar, molasses, and liquid smoke into the pot; bring to a simmer. Stir in collard greens gently. Reduce heat to low and simmer, covered, until tender, about 30 minutes.

NUTRITION FACTS:

238 calories; protein 10.3g; carbohydrates 35.1g; fat 7.5g;

Cheesy Rice Stuffed Jalapeno Poppers

Prep:
30 mins
Cook:
15 mins
Total:
45 mins
Servings:
12
Yield:
24 poppers

INGREDIENTS:

1 (8.8 ounce) pouch Original Long Grain or Whole Grain Brown
4 ounces cream cheese, softened
¼ cup shredded Mexican blend cheese
1 ½ teaspoons taco seasoning mix
1 teaspoon chopped fresh cilantro
12 large jalapeno peppers, halved lengthwise, seeds and membranes removed
1 cup panko bread crumbs
1 tablespoon melted butter

DIRECTIONS:

1

Preheat oven to 350 degrees F (175 degrees C). Line a baking sheet with parchment paper.

2

Prepare rice according to package directions. Allow to cool slightly.

3

Mix rice, cream cheese, shredded cheese, taco seasoning, and cilantro together in a bowl. Combine thoroughly.

4

Fill each jalapeno half with about a teaspoon of rice mixture, depending on size of jalapeno. Arrange filled jalapeno halves on prepared baking sheet.

5

Mix panko bread crumbs and melted butter together in a small bowl. Top filled jalapenos with crumb mixture.

6

Bake poppers in preheated oven until lightly golden on top, about 15 to 20 minutes.

NUTRITION FACTS:

108 calories; protein 2.9g; carbohydrates 13.6g; fat 5.7g;

Raisin and Spice Brown Rice

Prep:
10 mins
Cook:
45 mins
Total:
55 mins
Servings:
7
Yield:
3 1/2 cups

INGREDIENTS:

1 cup chopped onion
1 teaspoon minced fresh ginger
1 teaspoon ground cumin
½ teaspoon ground coriander
⅓ cup thinly sliced celery
¼ cup seedless raisins
1 tablespoon low-sodium soy sauce
freshly ground black pepper to taste
1 cup brown rice
2 cups chicken broth
1 tablespoon butter
1 bay leaf
1 tablespoon vegetable oil

DIRECTIONS:

1

Bring brown rice, chicken broth, butter, and bay leaf to a boil in a saucepan over high heat. Reduce heat to medium-low, cover, and simmer until the rice is tender, 45 to 50 minutes; discard bay leaf.

2

Meanwhile, heat the vegetable oil in a skillet over medium-high heat. Stir in onion and ginger; cook and stir until the onion begins to brown on the edges, about 3 minutes. Stir in the cumin and coriander, then stir in the celery and raisins. Reduce heat to medium, and cook until the celery becomes tender, about 5 minutes. Once ready, stir the onion mixture into the cooked rice along with the soy sauce; season to taste with pepper.

NUTRITION FACTS:

161 calories; protein 2.7g; carbohydrates 28.2g; fat 4.5g;

Hearts of Palm Risotto

Prep:
25 mins
Cook:
30 mins
Total:
55 mins
Servings:
2
Yield:
2 servings

INGREDIENTS:

¼ cup dry white wine
3 cups boiling vegetable broth
½ cup sliced hearts of palm
¼ cup grated Parmesan cheese
salt and pepper to taste
1 tablespoon chopped fresh parsley
1 tablespoon butter
1 tablespoon butter
1 tablespoon olive oil
½ cup finely chopped onion
⅔ cup Arborio rice

DIRECTIONS:

1

Heat 1 tablespoon of butter and olive oil in a large, heavy-bottomed saucepan over medium-high heat. Add the onion; cook and stir until it begins to turn golden brown at the edges, about 2 minutes. Pour in the rice and stir until the rice is coated in oil and has started to toast, 2 to 3 minutes. Reduce the heat to medium and stir in the white wine. Let it cook until it has mostly evaporated, then stir in one-third of the boiling vegetable broth; continue stirring until incorporated. Repeat this process twice more, stirring constantly. Incorporating the broth should take 15 to 20 minutes in all.

2

When the rice is mostly tender, but still has a very slight crunch, stir in the hearts of palm and Parmesan cheese; season with salt and pepper. Cook for another minute to heat through then stir in parsley and butter, and serve immediately.

NUTRITION FACTS:

573 calories; protein 12g; carbohydrates 75.2g; fat 22.2g;

Vegan Black Bean Burgers with Oats

Prep:
45 mins
Cook:
30 mins
Total:
1 hr 15 mins
Servings:
15
Yield:
15 burgers

INGREDIENTS:

1 white onion, cut into 1-inch pieces
3 tablespoons chopped fresh parsley
2 tablespoons vegan Worcestershire sauce
2 tablespoons salt, or more to taste
2 tablespoons ground black pepper
2 tablespoons onion powder
2 tablespoons garlic powder
1 tablespoon ground cumin
vegetable oil as needed
2 ½ cups canned black beans, liquid reserved
2 cups rolled oats, or more as needed
2 cups raw sunflower seed kernels
1 (16 ounce) package white mushrooms, stemmed and quartered
1 red bell pepper, cut into 1-inch pieces
1 green bell pepper, cut into 1-inch pieces

DIRECTIONS:

1

Process black beans in a food processor or blender with just enough of the reserved can liquid to get the processor going. Place into a large bowl.

2

Blend oats in the food processor until they become oat flour; add to the large bowl. Blend sunflower seeds until finely ground; add to the bowl. Blend mushrooms, bell peppers, and onion in batches in a food processor and add to oat mixture. Mix in parsley, Worcestershire, salt, pepper, onion powder, garlic powder, and cumin thoroughly using your hands or a rubber spatula, adding more processed oats if needed to hold shape.

3

Roll mixture into 15 tight balls, flatten, and cup the sides to ensure the patties do not have cracks. Place on wax or parchment paper.

4

Heat oil in a large skillet to 350 degrees F (175 degrees C), or over medium heat. Place patties carefully into the hot oil using your hands or a spatula, working in batches. Cook until browned and crispy, 3 to 5 minutes on each side. Remove and place onto a paper towel-lined plate to drain excess oil, about 2 minutes. Repeat with more oil until all burgers are cooked.

NUTRITION FACTS:

250 calories; protein 9.5g; carbohydrates 23.6g; fat 14.6g;

Tasty Chestnut, Lentils And Vegetable Stew

Prep:
15 mins
Cook:
1 hr 25 mins
Total:
1 hr 40 mins
Servings:
8
Yield:
8 servings

INGREDIENTS:

4 carrot, peeled and sliced
1 (32 fluid ounce) container vegetable broth
2 cups water
1 (15 ounce) can stewed tomatoes, undrained
1 (15 ounce) can brown lentils
2 (7 ounce) cans French chestnuts
1 pinch salt and ground black pepper to taste
3 tablespoons olive oil
½ onion, finely chopped
5 cloves garlic, minced
3 celery ribs, chopped

DIRECTIONS:

1

Pour the olive oil into a large, deep pot set over medium-high heat. Stir in the onion and garlic; cook until transparent, about 5 minutes. Add the celery, carrots, vegetable broth, and water; cook for 10 to 15 minutes. Reduce heat to medium, pour in the tomatoes, and cook 10 to 15 minutes more. Reduce heat to low, and mix in the lentils and chestnuts; cook for 1 hour until the chestnuts soften. Pour in more water to thin the stew, if desired. Season to taste with salt and pepper.

NUTRITION FACTS:

232 calories; protein 5.8g; carbohydrates 39g; fat 6.1g;

Sweet and Spicy Curry with Chickpeas

Prep:

15 mins

Cook:

30 mins

Total:

45 mins

Servings:

6

Yield:

6 servings

INGREDIENTS:

1 (14.5 ounce) can garbanzo beans (chickpeas), drained

1 (14.5 ounce) can diced tomatoes

2 tablespoons curry powder

½ cup bottled sweet chili sauce

½ cup coconut milk

salt and ground black pepper to taste

1 teaspoon red pepper flakes (Optional)

1 tablespoon sesame oil

2 pounds ground turkey thigh meat

1 onion, chopped

3 cloves garlic, pressed

DIRECTIONS:

1

Heat the sesame oil in a skillet over medium heat; cook the turkey with onion and garlic in the oil until the meat is no longer pink, 10 to 15 minutes. Chop the meat up into crumbles as it cooks. Stir in the garbanzo beans, tomatoes, curry powder, chili sauce, and coconut milk; bring the mixture to a boil. Reduce heat and simmer for 15 minutes. Season with salt, black pepper, and crushed red pepper flakes.

NUTRITION FACTS:

424 calories; protein 35.7g; carbohydrates 29.4g; fat 18.9g;

Amazing Red Beans And Rice

Prep:
10 mins
Cook:
3 hrs 55 mins
Additional:
8 hrs
Total:
12 hrs 5 mins
Servings:
6
Yield:
6 servings

INGREDIENTS:

1 pound dried red beans
3 andouille sausage links
1 slice ham steak, cubed, or more to taste
2 tablespoons Creole seasoning, divided
7 cups chicken broth
2 tablespoons chopped garlic
1 cup tomato sauce
2 teaspoons vinegar
½ cup chopped green onions, divided
2 tablespoons chopped fresh parsley
3 cups cooked rice, or to taste
2 tablespoons butter
2 cups minced onions
1 cup minced green bell pepper
½ cup minced celery
4 bay leaves

DIRECTIONS:

1

Place red beans into a large container and cover with several inches of cool water; let stand 8 hours to overnight. Drain.

2

Heat a skillet over medium heat; cook sausage until cooked through, 10 to 15 minutes. Transfer sausage to a work surface and slice.

3

Heat butter in a skillet over medium heat; cook and stir onions, bell pepper, celery, and bay leaves until softened, about 5 minutes. Add sausage, ham, and 1/2 of the Creole seasoning; saute over medium-high heat until lightly browned, about 10 minutes. Stir drained beans into sausage mixture.

4

Mix chicken broth, garlic, and remaining Creole seasoning into bean mixture; cover skillet and simmer on low for 3 hours.

5

Stir tomato sauce, vinegar, and 1/2 of the green onions into bean mixture, slightly smashing beans with a potato masher. Simmer, uncovered, until thickened and beans are tender, about 30 minutes more. Mix remaining green onions and parsley into beans and serve over cooked rice.

NUTRITION FACTS:

508 calories; protein 26.8g; carbohydrates 80.5g; fat 9.3g;

Maple Pecan Granola

Prep:
10 mins
Cook:
40 mins
Total:
50 mins
Servings:
18
Yield:
18 servings

INGREDIENTS:

2 teaspoons ground cinnamon
⅓ cup canola oil
⅔ cup pure maple syrup
1 teaspoon maple flavoring
¼ teaspoon salt
4 cups old-fashioned oats
½ cup chopped pecans
½ cup chopped walnuts
½ cup ground flax seed

DIRECTIONS:

1

Preheat the oven to 300 degrees F (150 degrees C).

2

Line a baking sheet with parchment paper.

3

Mix oats, pecans, walnuts, flax seed, and cinnamon in a large bowl.

4

Stir canola oil, maple syrup, maple flavoring, and salt together in a small bowl; pour over the oat mixture and stir to coat evenly.

5

Spread the resulting mixture evenly onto the prepared baking sheet.

6

Bake in the preheated oven until lightly browned, about 40 minutes.

7

Set granola aside to cool completely before breaking into chunks. Store in an air-tight container.

NUTRITION FACTS:

202 calories; protein 3.9g; carbohydrates 22.4g; fat 11.5g;

Smoky Black Bean Burgers

Prep:

10 mins

Cook:

10 mins

Additional:

35 mins

Total:

55 mins

Servings:

4

Yield:

4 burgers

INGREDIENTS:

1 clove garlic, minced

½ teaspoon salt

½ tablespoon Worcestershire sauce

⅛ teaspoon liquid smoke flavoring

cooking spray

1 tablespoon ground flax seed

3 tablespoons water

1 (15 ounce) can black beans - drained, rinsed, and mashed

¼ cup panko bread crumbs

DIRECTIONS:

1

Mix ground flax seed and water together in a small bowl. Let sit to thicken, about 5 minutes.

2

Mix flax mixture, black beans, panko bread crumbs, garlic, salt, Worcestershire sauce, and liquid smoke together in a bowl until combined. Form batter into 4 patties; arrange on a plate. Chill in refrigerator until set, about 30 minutes.

3

Spray a skillet with cooking spray; place patties in skillet over medium heat. Cook until browned, about 5 minutes per side.

NUTRITION FACTS:

128 calories; protein 7.5g; carbohydrates 23.4g; fat 1.5g;

Whitney Hayes

Fried Polenta Squares with Creamy Mushroom Ragu

Prep:
2 hrs 30 mins
Cook:
1 hr 15 mins
Total:
3 hrs 45 mins
Servings:
4
Yield:
4 servings

INGREDIENTS:

1 small yellow onion, diced
3 cloves garlic, minced
1 pound mixed wild mushrooms (like shiitake, oyster, chanterelle, hen of the woods), cleaned and sliced
1 pound cremini mushrooms, cleaned and sliced
1 tablespoon minced fresh thyme
2 tablespoons all-purpose flour
½ cup dry white wine
¼ cup heavy cream
1 teaspoon sugar
1 squeeze fresh lemon juice

205

½ cup chopped flat-leaf parsley
1 sheet Wrap Aluminum Foil
4 cups water
1 cup polenta
½ cup finely grated Parmesan cheese
¾ teaspoon kosher salt, divided
2 tablespoons olive oil

DIRECTIONS:

1

Bring 4 cups of water to a boil. Whisk in the polenta. Once it begins to thicken, reduce heat to a simmer and cook for 45 minutes until creamy and thick, stirring occasionally to prevent sticking. Stir in the Parmesan and a 1/4 teaspoon of salt. Stir until melted and cheese is no longer visible. Remove from heat.

2

Line an 8x11 inch baking dish with Reynolds Wrap® Aluminum Foil and carefully pour the polenta into the baking dish, using a spatula to smooth it to an even thickness, about 3/4 inch. Cover and refrigerate for at least two hours and up to two days until firm.

3

While the polenta chills, make your ragu. In a large heavy skillet, heat the olive oil over medium heat until shimmering. Add the onion and garlic and saute until fragrant and translucent, about 5 minutes. Stir often to prevent browning. Add mushrooms and thyme and cook over medium-high heat until the mushrooms start to release their liquid. Add 1/2 teaspoon of salt and continue to cook another 5 minutes until they begin to soften more.

4

Add flour, stirring, until it is no longer visible, about 1 minute. Add in the wine, cream and sugar, and bring the mixture to a simmer. Taste and adjust salt if desired. Simmer until thick and creamy and the mushrooms are nicely coated, about 15 minutes. Finish with a squeeze of fresh lemon juice and 1/2 cup minced parsley. Set aside and cover to keep warm.

5

Slice your polenta into squares -- whatever size you desire. Wipe down your skillet, coat it with nonstick cooking spray, and heat it over medium-high. Fry the squares in the pan until golden brown and warmed through. To serve, top the squares with warm mushroom ragu.

NUTRITION FACTS:

448 calories; protein 19g; carbohydrates 46.9g; fat 19g;

Quick Brown Rice and Mushroom Pilaf

Servings:

8

Yield:

8 servings

INGREDIENTS:

2 tablespoons olive oil

1 small onion, chopped

¼ cup celery, chopped

1 ½ cups sliced mushrooms

1 (14.5 ounce) can chicken broth

2 cups Brown Rice, uncooked

½ cup chopped walnuts, toasted

2 tablespoons fresh parsley, chopped

DIRECTIONS:

1

Heat oil in medium saucepan on medium heat. Add onions and celery; cook 3 minutes or until crisp-tender, stirring occasionally.

2

Add mushrooms; cook 3 minutes or until mushrooms are tender, stirring occasionally. Add broth; stir. Bring to boil.

3

Stir in rice; cover. Reduce heat to medium-low; simmer 5 minutes. Remove from heat; let stand 5 minutes. Add walnuts and parsley; mix lightly.

NUTRITION FACTS:
163 calories; protein 3.4g; carbohydrates 19.7g; fat 9.1g;

Fantastic Roasted Veggie Buddha Bowl

Prep:
25 mins
Cook:
42 mins
Total:
1 hr 7 mins
Servings:
2
Yield:
2 bowls

INGREDIENTS:

1 cup water
½ cup bulgur
1 sweet potato, peeled and cut into 1-inch cubes
4 teaspoons olive oil, divided
salt and ground black pepper to taste
½ pound fennel bulb, trimmed and cut into 1-inch cubes
1 small red onion, cut into 1-inch pieces
1 red bell pepper, cut into 1-inch strips
1 (8 ounce) package tempeh, cut into 1-inch pieces
½ teaspoon curry powder
2 teaspoons coconut oil

Orange-Curry Dressing:

¼ cup fresh squeezed orange juice
2 tablespoons olive oil
2 teaspoons red wine vinegar
½ teaspoon curry powder
¼ teaspoon salt
¼ teaspoon ground black pepper
2 tablespoons raw pumpkin seeds (pepitas)

DIRECTIONS:

1

Preheat oven to 400 degrees F (200 degrees C). Line a baking sheet with parchment paper.

2

Bring water and bulgur to a boil in a saucepan; cover and reduce heat to medium-low. Simmer until water is absorbed and bulgur is soft, about 12 minutes. Keep warm.

3

Place sweet potato in a bowl and drizzle 1 teaspoon olive oil over it; season with salt and pepper. Toss to coat. Transfer sweet potato to the prepared baking sheet, placing in 1 row. Place fennel in the same bowl, add 1 teaspoon olive oil, and season with salt and pepper. Toss to coat and place fennel next to sweet potato, keeping each separate.

4

Roast in the preheated oven for 10 minutes. Place red onion in the same bowl; add 1 teaspoon olive oil, and season with salt and pepper. Toss to coat and place on the baking sheet with sweet potato and fennel, keeping them separate. Place red bell pepper in the same bowl; add 1 teaspoon olive oil, and season with salt and pepper. Toss to coat and place on the baking sheet next to the onion.

5

Roast in the oven until all the vegetables are cooked to desired doneness, 10 to 15 minutes.

6

Place tempeh in a bowl and season with 1/2 teaspoon curry powder, tossing to coat.

7

Heat coconut oil in a skillet over medium-high heat; saute tempeh, turning occasionally, until all sides are evenly browned, about 10 minutes.

8

Whisk orange juice, 2 tablespoons olive oil, red wine vinegar, 1/2 teaspoon curry powder, 1/4 teaspoon salt, and 1/4 teaspoon pepper in a small bowl until dressing is smooth.

9

Divide bulgur between 2 bowls. Place half of sweet potato, fennel, red onion, and red bell pepper around bulgur; top each with 1 tablespoon pumpkin seeds. Drizzle dressing over each bowl.

NUTRITION FACTS:

835 calories; protein 32.2g; carbohydrates 86.7g; fat 44.8g;

Vegan Sweet Potato Chili

Prep:
15 mins
Cook:
1 hr 10 mins
Total:
1 hr 25 mins
Servings:
6
Yield:
6 servings

INGREDIENTS:

1 tablespoon ground cumin
½ teaspoon smoked paprika
½ teaspoon dried oregano
½ teaspoon red pepper flakes
1 ½ teaspoons tomato paste
2 cups vegetable broth
1 (28 ounce) can diced tomatoes
2 cups drained and rinsed kidney beans
5 tablespoons vegetable broth
½ cup chopped onion
3 cloves garlic, minced
½ jalapeno pepper, minced
2 sweet potatoes, diced
2 tablespoons chili powder

DIRECTIONS:

1

Heat 5 tablespoons vegetable broth in a large skillet over medium heat. Cook and stir onion, garlic, and jalapeno pepper in the hot broth until slightly tender, about 5 minutes. Add sweet potatoes, chili powder, cumin, paprika, oregano, and red pepper flakes to onion mixture. Pour remaining 2 cups vegetable broth over sweet potato mixture.

2

Bring vegetable broth mixture to a boil, reduce heat to medium, and simmer until sweet potatoes are tender, 20 to 25 minutes. Stir tomatoes and kidney beans into sweet potato mixture and simmer over low heat until flavors have blended, about 45 minutes.

NUTRITION FACTS:

215 calories; protein 8.4g; carbohydrates 42.7g; fat 1.4g;

Seasoned Roasted Root Vegetables

Prep:
30 mins
Cook:
45 mins
Total:
1 hr 15 mins
Servings:
10
Yield:
10 servings

INGREDIENTS:

Olive oil cooking spray
1 butternut squash - peeled, seeded, and cut into 1-inch pieces
1 large sweet potato, peeled and cut into 1-inch cubes
1 (10 ounce) package frozen Brussels sprouts, thawed and halved
1 onion, halved and thickly sliced
1 parsnip, peeled and sliced
3 carrots, cut into large chunks
2 tablespoons olive oil, or as needed
1 teaspoon ground thyme
1 teaspoon dried rosemary
1 pinch salt
ground black pepper to taste

DIRECTIONS:

1

Preheat oven to 400 degrees F (200 degrees C). Spray a baking sheet with cooking spray.

2

Combine butternut squash, sweet potato, Brussels sprouts, onion, parsnip, and carrots in a large bowl. Drizzle with olive oil and toss to coat. Add thyme, rosemary, salt, and black pepper; toss again. Transfer coated vegetables to the prepared baking sheet.

3

Roast vegetables in the preheated oven for 25 minutes; stir and continue roasting until vegetables are slightly brown and tender, about 20 more minutes.

NUTRITION FACTS:

149 calories; protein 3.4g; carbohydrates 29.9g; fat 3.1g;

Grilled Portobello Mushrooms with Blue Cheese

Prep:
5 mins
Cook:
20 mins
Total:
25 mins
Servings:
4
Yield:
4 servings

INGREDIENTS:

4 portobello mushrooms, stems removed
4 ounces crumbled blue cheese

DIRECTIONS:

1
Preheat an outdoor grill for medium-high heat and lightly oil the grate.

2
Place mushrooms, gill-side up, on a work surface; fill each with 1 ounce blue cheese.

3
Cook mushrooms, blue cheese-side up, on the preheated grill, rotating every 5 minutes, until mushrooms are tender and cheese is melted, about 20 minutes.

NUTRITION FACTS:

129 calories; protein 8.9g; carbohydrates 6.3g; fat 8.4g;

Easy Avocado And Egg Burrito

Prep:
15 mins
Cook:
5 mins
Total:
20 mins
Servings:
2
Yield:
2 burritos

INGREDIENTS:

1 Hass avocado - peeled, pitted, and sliced
1 small tomato, chopped
1 small bunch fresh cilantro, chopped, or to taste (Optional)
1 pinch salt and ground black pepper to taste
1 dash hot sauce, or to taste (Optional)
2 (10 inch) flour tortillas
1 tablespoon butter
4 medium eggs
1 cup shredded mild Cheddar cheese

DIRECTIONS:

1

Place tortillas on a microwave-safe plate. Place shredded Cheddar cheese in the center of each tortilla, towards 1 end. Microwave on high power to melt cheese, 20 to 30 seconds.

2

Heat butter in a skillet over medium heat. Whisk eggs together in a bowl. Pour into the skillet; cook and stir until eggs are set, about 5 minutes.

3

Place eggs over melted cheese on tortillas; top each with avocado, tomato, and cilantro. Season with salt and pepper. Top with hot sauce.

NUTRITION FACTS:

863 calories; protein 38.3g; carbohydrates 48.5g; fat 58.9g;

Grilled Fruit Kabobs

Prep:
15 mins
Cook:
20 mins
Total:
35 mins
Servings:
6
Yield:
12 kabobs

INGREDIENTS:

3 fresh plums, pitted and quartered
3 bananas, cut into 4 pieces each
12 strawberries, hulled
12 skewers
½ cup margarine
¼ cup honey
3 fresh peaches, pitted and quartered

DIRECTIONS:

1

Preheat an outdoor grill for medium heat and place a large sheet of foil onto the grate.

2

Melt the margarine and honey together in a small saucepan over medium heat. Reduce heat to low and cook gently, stirring occasionally, until slightly thickened, about 5 minutes. Do not let the sauce boil.

3

Thread a peach quarter, a plum quarter, a banana piece, and a strawberry onto each skewer. Place the skewers onto the foil on the preheated grill; spoon margarine-honey mixture over each skewer.

4

Grill until the fruit is softened and the sauce has thickened and cooked onto the fruit, about 5 minutes. Flip the skewers, spoon more margarine-honey sauce over each, and grill for about 5 more minutes on the other side.

NUTRITION FACTS:

268 calories; protein 1.3g; carbohydrates 34.8g; fat 15.4g

Zucchini, Squash, and Corn Casserole

Prep:
20 mins
Cook:
1 hr
Total:
1 hr 20 mins
Servings:
16
Yield:
1 9x13-inch casserole

INGREDIENTS:

1 ½ cups shredded sharp white Cheddar cheese
1 cup grated Asiago cheese, divided
1 ½ cups bread crumbs, divided
½ cup mayonnaise
2 large eggs, beaten
1 teaspoon salt
1 teaspoon ground black pepper
1 pound yellow squash, cut into 1/4-inch slices
1 pound zucchini, cut into 1/4-inch slices
4 tablespoons butter, divided
2 cups diced sweet onion
2 cloves garlic, minced
1 (15.25 ounce) can whole kernel corn, drained
1 (15 ounce) can cream-style corn

DIRECTIONS:

1

Preheat the oven to 350 degrees F (175 degrees C). Grease a 9x13-inch casserole dish.

2

Combine zucchini and squash in a large pan, add water to cover, and boil for 5 minutes over medium-high heat. Drain and gently press zucchini and squash between paper towels to remove excess water.

3

Meanwhile, melt 2 tablespoons butter in a skillet. Add onion and saute for 2 minutes. Add garlic and cook until onion has softened and garlic is fragrant, 2 more minutes. Mix in zucchini and squash. Add whole kernel corn, cream-style corn, Cheddar cheese, 1/2 cup Asiago cheese, 1/2 cup breadcrumbs, mayonnaise, eggs, salt, and pepper. Pour into the prepared casserole dish.

4

Melt remaining 2 tablespoons butter in a skillet. Add remaining 1 cup breadcrumbs and remaining 1/2 cup Asiago cheese. Mix well and sprinkle on top of the casserole.

5

Bake in the preheated oven until casserole is golden and set and cheese is melted, 45 to 50 minutes.

NUTRITION FACTS:

253 calories; protein 8.7g; carbohydrates 22.4g; fat 15.5g;

Vegetarian Garden Stir-Fry

Prep:
15 mins
Cook:
10 mins
Total:
25 mins
Servings:
3
Yield:
3 servings

INGREDIENTS:

2 tablespoons chia seeds
2 teaspoons cayenne pepper, or to taste
1 tablespoon garlic, minced
salt to taste
3 tablespoons egg whites
2 tablespoons shredded Cheddar cheese, or as desired
1 serving cooking spray
½ cup sugar snap peas
¼ cup cherry tomatoes, halved
½ cup dried fruit and nut mix, such as cranberries, almonds, and cashews
¼ cup chopped mushrooms
¼ cup bell pepper, thinly sliced

DIRECTIONS:

1

Grease a large skillet with cooking spray and heat over medium-low heat. Add sugar snap peas, cherry tomatoes, fruit and nut mix, mushrooms, bell pepper, and chia seeds. Stir-fry about 2 minutes. Season with cayenne, garlic, and salt. Cook and stir about 2 minutes more.

2

Stir in egg whites slowly, mixing until they are cooked through, but not crusty, 3 to 5 minutes. Transfer stir-fry to a large bowl and sprinkle with Cheddar cheese. Let cheese melt and serve.

NUTRITION FACTS:

158 calories; protein 6.3g; carbohydrates 25.6g; fat 4.5g;

Tasty Ratatouille Provencale

Prep:
15 mins
Cook:
1 hr 5 mins
Total:
1 hr 20 mins
Servings:
6
Yield:
6 servings

INGREDIENTS:

2 pounds fresh tomatoes, quartered
3 eggplants, sliced into 1/2-inch rounds
6 zucchini, sliced 1/2-inch thick
½ cup tomato puree (Optional)
3 tablespoons herbes de Provence
salt and ground black pepper to taste
½ cup extra-virgin olive oil
2 large onions, quartered
3 cloves garlic, minced

DIRECTIONS:

1

Pour olive oil into a large pot over high heat. Add onions and garlic and saute for 2 minutes. Reduce heat and add tomatoes, eggplants, zucchini, tomato puree, herbes de Provence, salt, and pepper. Cover and simmer for 30 minutes.

2

Uncover and check the level of liquid in the pot. Continue cooking for 30 minutes, uncovered if there is too much liquid, or covered if the amount of liquid looks right.

NUTRITION FACTS:

323 calories; protein 7.5g; carbohydrates 35.2g; fat 19.9g;

Vegetarian Veggie Casserole

Prep:
30 mins
Cook:
31 mins
Additional:
5 mins
Total:
1 hr 6 mins
Servings:
6
Yield:
6 servings

INGREDIENTS:

Casserole:
3 potatoes
1 tablespoon olive oil (Optional)
¼ cup chopped onion (Optional)
1 (14.5 ounce) can cut green beans
1 (10 ounce) package frozen carrot, peas, and corn blend
1 (10 ounce) package frozen lima beans

Cashew Gravy:
3 cups water, divided
½ cup unsalted raw cashews
2 tablespoons liquid aminos (such as Bragg®)
2 tablespoons cornstarch
2 teaspoons onion powder
½ teaspoon ground white pepper, or to taste
¼ teaspoon garlic powder, or more to taste

Drop Biscuits:

2 cups baking mix (such as Arrowhead Mills®)

⅔ cup almond milk

2 tablespoons vegetable oil

½ teaspoon salt

DIRECTIONS:

1

Pierce potatoes in several places with a sharp knife. Cook in the microwave, turning once, until tender, about 10 minutes. Cool until easily handled, about 5 minutes. Peel and cut into cubes.

2

Preheat oven to 425 degrees F (220 degrees C). Grease a 9x13-inch baking dish.

3

Heat olive oil in a small skillet over medium heat. Cook and stir onion in the hot oil until golden, 5 to 10 minutes. Remove from heat.

4

Combine potato cubes, onion, green beans, frozen carrot blend, and frozen lima beans in a large bowl. Toss gently to mix together. Spread in the prepared baking dish.

5

Combine 1 1/2 cup water, cashews, liquid aminos, cornstarch, onion powder, white pepper, and garlic powder in a high-powered blender; blend until completely smooth. Add remaining 1 1/2 cup water; blend until thoroughly incorporated.

6

Pour cashew mixture into a saucepan over medium-high heat; cook, stirring constantly, until gravy is slightly thickened, about 5 minutes.

7

Pour gravy into the baking dish; spread with a spatula to coat vegetables evenly. Cover with aluminum foil.

8

Bake in the preheated oven until gravy just starts to bubble, about 12 minutes.

9

Stir baking mix, almond milk, vegetable oil, and salt in a bowl until dough is just moistened. Uncover baking dish and drop spoonfuls of biscuit dough over the gravy.

10

Return to the oven and bake, uncovered, until biscuits turn golden brown, 14 to 16 minutes.

NUTRITION FACTS:

488 calories; protein 12.8g; carbohydrates 70.3g; fat 18.7g;

Vegetable Patties

Prep:
10 mins
Cook:
30 mins
Total:
40 mins
Servings:
6
Yield:
6 servings

INGREDIENTS:

1 teaspoon ground coriander
½ cup frozen green peas, thawed
2 fresh green chile peppers
salt to taste
¼ teaspoon chili powder
½ teaspoon lemon juice
1 (8 ounce) can refrigerated crescent roll dough
2 baking potatoes, peeled and cubed
2 tablespoons vegetable oil
½ teaspoon cumin seeds
½ teaspoon ground turmeric

DIRECTIONS:

1

Preheat oven to 350 degrees F (175 degrees C).

2

Bring a large pot of salted water to a boil. Add potatoes and cook until tender but still firm, about 15 minutes; drain.

3

In a medium saucepan over medium-low heat, heat oil and add cumin seeds. As they begin to sputter add turmeric and coriander, then potatoes, peas and green chile peppers. Stir in salt and chili powder; cook, stirring occasionally, for 5 minutes. Stir in lemon juice.

4

Roll out crescent dough; fill each roll with potato mixture and form into patties.

5

Bake in a preheated oven for 20 minutes, or until evenly browned.

NUTRITION FACTS:

260 calories; protein 4.8g; carbohydrates 31g; fat 12.8g;

Carrot Pecan Crunch Pie

Servings:

8

Yield:

1 pie

INGREDIENTS:

4 cups carrots, cut into 1 inch pieces

2 eggs

1 (14 ounce) can sweetened condensed milk

1 teaspoon pumpkin pie spice

1 pinch salt

1 (9 inch) unbaked pie shell

½ cup packed brown sugar

¼ cup butter, melted

1 cup chopped pecans

DIRECTIONS:

1

Preheat oven to 375 degrees F (190 degrees C).

2

To Make Topping: In a medium bowl combine brown sugar, melted butter or margarine, and chopped pecans. Mix well and set aside.

3

To Make Carrot Custard: Steam carrots until tender. Drain and cool. Place cooled carrots in a blender or food processor and add eggs, condensed milk, pumpkin pie spice, and salt. Blend until smooth. Pour carrot mixture into pie shell. Sprinkle with pecan topping.

4

Bake in preheated oven for 45 minutes or until toothpick inserted in center comes out clean.

NUTRITION FACTS:

523 calories; protein 8.4g; carbohydrates 60.2g; fat 29.2g;

Apple Slaw With Pineapple

Prep:
15 mins
Total:
15 mins
Servings:
12
Yield:
12 servings

INGREDIENTS:

4 cups finely shredded cabbage
1 large red apple, cored and diced
1 (8 ounce) can crushed pineapple, drained
½ cup heavy whipping cream
½ cup mayonnaise
1 tablespoon white sugar

DIRECTIONS:

1
Whisk cream, mayonnaise, and sugar in a large salad bowl until sugar
has dissolved. Gently fold in cabbage, apple, and pineapple to coat
with dressing. Refrigerate until serving time.

NUTRITION FACTS:

103 calories; protein 0.7g; carbohydrates 10.4g; fat 7g;

Spaghetti Aglio e Olio

Prep:
10 mins
Cook:
22 mins
Total:
32 mins
Servings:
4
Yield:
4 servings

INGREDIENTS:

¼ teaspoon red pepper flakes, or to taste
salt and freshly ground black pepper to taste
¼ cup chopped fresh Italian parsley
1 cup finely grated Parmigiano-Reggiano cheese
1 pound uncooked spaghetti
6 cloves garlic, thinly sliced
½ cup olive oil

DIRECTIONS:

1

Bring a large pot of lightly salted water to a boil. Cook spaghetti in the boiling water, stirring occasionally until cooked through but firm to the bite, about 12 minutes. Drain and transfer to a pasta bowl.

2

Combine garlic and olive oil in a cold skillet. Cook over medium heat to slowly toast garlic, about 10 minutes. Reduce heat to medium-low when olive oil begins to bubble. Cook and stir until garlic is golden brown, about another 5 minutes. Remove from heat.

3

Stir red pepper flakes, black pepper, and salt into the pasta. Pour in olive oil and garlic, and sprinkle on Italian parsley and half of the Parmigiano-Reggiano cheese; stir until combined.

4

Serve pasta topped with the remaining Parmigiano-Reggiano cheese.

NUTRITION FACTS:

755 calories; protein 22.9g; carbohydrates 87.4g; fat 34.5g;

Vegan Gnocchi with Pesto, Spinach, and Cannellini Beans

Prep:

10 mins

Cook:

25 mins

Total:

35 mins

Servings:

5

Yield:

5 servings

INGREDIENTS:

1 (15 ounce) can cannellini beans

⅓ cup french-fried onions

¼ cup white wine

½ teaspoon kosher salt

½ teaspoon dried sage

¾ cup vegan pesto

½ cup vegetable broth

1 cup frozen chopped spinach

1 (16 ounce) package gnocchi

4 tablespoons olive oil, divided

1 (8 ounce) package crimini mushrooms, quartered

3 stalks celery, diced

DIRECTIONS:

1

Place spinach in a microwave-safe dish. Cover and microwave on high for 4 minutes. Separate with a fork and drain.

2

Bring a large pot of lightly salted water to a boil. Cook gnocchi in the boiling water until they float to the top, 2 to 4 minutes. Drain and set aside.

3

Meanwhile, heat 2 tablespoons olive oil in a large skillet over medium heat until warm. Add mushrooms and cook until they begin to soften, about 3 minutes. Add celery, cover, and cook for 3 more minutes. Remove mushrooms and celery to a bowl.

4

Heat remaining 2 tablespoons olive oil in the skillet. Add gnocchi and brown, flipping halfway through, 4 to 6 minutes. Add mushroom-celery mixture, cannellini beans, spinach, onions, wine, salt, and sage; simmer until heated through, about 3 minutes.

5

Mix together vegan pesto and vegetable broth in a small bowl. Pour into skillet over gnocchi and serve.

NUTRITION FACTS:

531 calories; protein 10g; carbohydrates 41.3g; fat 35.6g;

Asian Rice Noodle Salad

Prep:
20 mins
Cook:
15 mins
Total:
35 mins
Servings:
8
Yield:
8 servings

INGREDIENTS:

8 ounces rice noodles
1 pound lean ground pork
1 cup thinly sliced green onions
1 cup chopped cilantro
1 cup thinly sliced snow peas
1 large red onion, quartered and thinly sliced
¼ cup roasted peanuts
⅓ cup low sodium soy sauce
⅓ cup seasoned rice wine vinegar
¼ cup lime juice
2 tablespoons chile paste with garlic
1 tablespoon sesame oil
1 tablespoon minced fresh ginger root
1 teaspoon dried mint

DIRECTIONS:

1

Combine soy sauce, rice wine vinegar, lime juice, chile paste with garlic, sesame oil, ginger root, and mint in a jar with a tight-fitting lid; cover and shake until sauce is well blended.

2

Bring a large pot of water to a boil; add noodles and cook until tender, about 5 minutes. Drain, cool, and place in a serving bowl. Cut noodles using kitchen shears.

3

Heat a large skillet over medium-high heat. Cook and stir pork in the hot skillet until browned and crumbly, 5 to 7 minutes; drain, discard grease, and cool on paper towels. Add pork to noodles.

4

Mix green onions, cilantro, snow peas, and red onion with pork and noodles.

5

Place peanuts in a heavy resealable bag; seal and lightly crush using the bottom of a jar or large glass. Add peanuts to noodle mixture. Add sauce and toss well.

NUTRITION FACTS:

304 calories; protein 13.7g; carbohydrates 33.8g; fat 12.9g;

Spaghetti Sauce with Fresh Tomatoes

Prep:
15 mins
Cook:
1 hr 10 mins
Total:
1 hr 25 mins
Servings:
8
Yield:
1 quart sauce

INGREDIENTS:

1 tablespoon white sugar
1 tablespoon dried basil
1 tablespoon dried parsley
1 teaspoon salt
¼ cup olive oil
1 onion, chopped
½ teaspoon garlic powder
4 pounds fresh tomatoes, peeled and chopped

DIRECTIONS:

1

Heat olive oil in a large skillet over medium heat. Add onion and garlic powder; cook and stir until onion is translucent, about 5 minutes. Add tomatoes, sugar, basil, parsley, and salt. Bring to a boil. Reduce heat and simmer, stirring occasionally, until sauce thickens, 1 to 2 hours.

NUTRITION FACTS:

120 calories; protein 2.5g; carbohydrates 13.5g; fat 7.3g;

Teriyaki Eggs

Prep:

10 mins

Cook:

8 mins

Additional:

6 hrs 15 mins

Total:

6 hrs 33 mins

Servings:

6

Yield:

6 eggs

INGREDIENTS:

6 tablespoons white sugar

1 tablespoon dried minced onion

½ teaspoon sesame oil

6 eggs

½ cup soy sauce

½ cup water

DIRECTIONS:

1

Place eggs in a large saucepan and cover with cold water. Bring to a boil; remove from heat, cover, and let sit until eggs are cooked through, about 10 minutes. Drain hot water; cover eggs with cold water.

2

Peel eggs and place in a quart-size Mason jar.

3

Combine soy sauce, water, sugar, minced onion, and sesame oil in a saucepan over medium heat. Cook and stir until sugar is dissolved, 3 to 5 minutes. Cool briefly, about 5 minutes. Pour over eggs in the jar.

4

Refrigerate eggs until flavors are absorbed, at least 6 hours.

NUTRITION FACTS:

137 calories; protein 7.7g; carbohydrates 15g; fat 5.4g;

Vegan Stir-Fry Noodles

Prep:
20 mins
Cook:
15 mins
Total:
35 mins
Servings:
2
Yield:
2 servings

INGREDIENTS:

6 leaves bok choy, chopped
2 tablespoons soy sauce
1 teaspoon teriyaki sauce
ground black pepper to taste
1 teaspoon sesame oil
1 green onion, finely chopped
½ (8 ounce) package dried soba noodles
1 tablespoon oil, or as needed
¼ cup onion
2 cloves garlic, finely chopped
1 cup assorted mushrooms
¼ cup chopped eggplant

DIRECTIONS:

1

Bring a large pot of lightly salted water to a boil. Cook soba in boiling water, stirring occasionally, until noodles are tender yet firm to the bite, 5 to 6 minutes. Drain.

2

Heat oil in a large skillet over medium heat. Add onion and garlic and stir-fry for 1 minute. Toss in mushrooms and eggplant; cook for 2 minutes more. Add cooked soba noodles, bok choy, soy sauce, teriyaki sauce, and pepper. Cook until bok choy is tender, about 2 minutes.

3

Sprinkle sesame oil and green onion over vegetables and serve.

NUTRITION FACTS:

326 calories; protein 12.2g; carbohydrates 53g; fat 10g;

Amazing Noodle Veggie Bowl

Prep:

15 mins

Cook:

10 mins

Total:

25 mins

Servings:

1

Yield:

1 serving

INGREDIENTS:

1 tablespoon olive oil

½ green bell pepper, chopped

¼ onion, sliced

½ cup fresh green beans, trimmed and cut into 1 1/2-inch pieces

1 cup baby spinach leaves

3 ounces dried soba noodles

2 tablespoons soy sauce

2 tablespoons oyster sauce

1 tablespoon mirin (Japanese sweet wine)

DIRECTIONS:

1

Fill a large pot with lightly salted water and bring to a rolling boil. Drop in soba noodles and return to a boil. Cook uncovered, stirring occasionally, until tender yet firm to the bite, about 7 minutes. Drain.

2

Meanwhile, combine soy sauce, oyster sauce, and mirin in a small bowl. Set aside.

3

Heat olive oil in a skillet over medium-high heat. Add bell pepper, onion, and green beans and saute until softened but still crisp, 2 to 3 minutes. Add soba noodles and toss with the cooked vegetables. Mix in soy sauce mixture and cook for an additional 1 to 2 minutes. Add baby spinach and cook until desired doneness, 2 to 3 minutes. Serve in a bowl.

NUTRITION FACTS:

503 calories; protein 16.9g; carbohydrates 81g; fat 14.4g;

Creamy Vegan Pumpkin Penne Pasta

Prep:
25 mins
Cook:
1 hr 25 mins
Additional:
4 hrs 10 mins
Total:
6 hrs
Servings:
12
Yield:
12 servings

INGREDIENTS:

1 teaspoon dried basil
½ teaspoon oregano
sea salt and ground black pepper to taste
2 (16 ounce) packages penne pasta
¼ cup fresh basil, or to taste
1 ½ cups raw cashews
9 teaspoons extra-virgin olive oil, divided
1 small sugar pie pumpkin, halved and seeded
5 fresh sage leaves
1 yellow onion, chopped
5 cloves garlic, minced
½ cup unsweetened coconut milk
1 cup tomato sauce

DIRECTIONS:

1

Place cashews in a bowl and cover with water. Soak 4 hours to overnight. Drain and rinse cashews.

2

Preheat the oven to 350 degrees F (175 degrees C).

3

Drizzle 3 tablespoons oil in a baking dish and add pumpkin, cut-sides down. Pierce a few holes in the skin using a fork. Cover with aluminum foil.

4

Bake in the preheated oven for 40 minutes. Add sage leaves to the baking dish with the pumpkin, replace aluminum foil, and bake until pumpkin is very tender, about 5 minutes more. Remove from oven and keep covered; let pumpkin and sage continue to steam 10 to 15 minutes more.

5

Heat 2 tablespoons olive oil in a large skillet over medium heat. Add onion and garlic; cook and stir until golden brown, 3 to 5 minutes. Add tomato sauce, steamed sage leaves, dried basil, oregano, and salt. Cook and stir until incorporated, about 10 minutes. Scrape pumpkin flesh into skillet. Add coconut milk. Simmer 15 to 20 minutes more. Remove and discard sage leaves.

6

Fill blender halfway with tomato mixture and add 1/2 the soaked cashews. Season generously with salt and pepper. Cover and hold lid down with a potholder; pulse a few times before leaving on to blend until smooth and creamy. Add remaining 4 tablespoons olive oil and blend again. Pour into a pot. Repeat with remaining tomato mixture. Adjust seasoning if necessary.

7

Bring a large pot of lightly salted water to a boil. Add penne and cook, stirring occasionally, until tender yet firm to the bite, about 11 minutes. Drain, reserving 1/2 cup pasta water. Return pasta to the pot.

8

Stir 1/2 the sauce into the pot with the cooked pasta. Add more as needed to coat. Add reserved pasta water, 1/4 cup at a time, to thin sauce to desired creamy consistency. Add remaining sauce as desired. Top with fresh basil and serve hot.

NUTRITION FACTS:

441 calories; protein 13.7g; carbohydrates 66.1g; fat 15.3g;

Vegan Chickpea Noodle Soup

Prep:
10 mins
Cook:
10 mins
Total:
20 mins
Servings:
4
Yield:
4 servings

INGREDIENTS:

1 teaspoon onion powder
¾ teaspoon garlic granules
½ teaspoon ground turmeric
¼ teaspoon paprika
½ (8 ounce) package angel hair pasta
4 cups water
1 (14 ounce) can chickpeas, drained
½ cup sliced white mushrooms
5 tablespoons nutritional yeast
4 tablespoons minced fresh parsley
1 teaspoon salt
1 teaspoon toasted sesame oil

DIRECTIONS:

1

Combine water, chickpeas, mushrooms, nutritional yeast, parsley, salt, sesame oil, onion powder, garlic granules, turmeric, and paprika in a large saucepan over high heat. Bring to a boil. Add angel hair pasta and cook in the boiling water, stirring occasionally, until tender yet firm to the bite, 4 to 5 minutes.

2

Remove from heat, taste, and adjust seasoning if needed. Ladle into warmed bowls.

NUTRITION FACTS:

249 calories; protein 13.6g; carbohydrates 42.8g; fat 3.6g;

Penne with Spring Vegetables

Prep:
10 mins
Cook:
15 mins
Total:
25 mins
Servings:
4
Yield:
4 servings

INGREDIENTS:

3 tablespoons olive oil
½ cup grated Parmesan cheese
salt and pepper to taste
1 pound fresh asparagus, trimmed and cut into 1/2 inch pieces
1 (8 ounce) package sugar snap peas, trimmed
1 (8 ounce) package dry penne pasta

DIRECTIONS:

1

Bring a large pot of lightly salted water to a boil. Add asparagus, and cook for 2 minutes. Add peas, and cook for 2 more minutes. Transfer to a large bowl; set aside. Add pasta to boiling water, and cook for 8 to 10 minutes or until al dente; drain.

2

Place pasta in the bowl with asparagus and peas. Toss with olive oil, Parmesan, salt and pepper.

NUTRITION FACTS:

383 calories; protein 15.2g; carbohydrates 50.4g; fat 14.4g;

Roasted Cherry Tomato Sauce with Spaghetti

Prep:
15 mins
Cook:
45 mins
Additional:
10 mins
Total:
1 hr 10 mins
Servings:
6
Yield:
6 servings

INGREDIENTS:

2 pints cherry tomatoes
salt and ground black pepper to taste
1 pound fresh mozzarella cheese, cut into 1/2-inch cubes
¼ cup fresh basil, cut into strips
1 head garlic
2 drizzles extra-virgin olive oil, divided
1 (16 ounce) package spaghetti

DIRECTIONS:

1

Preheat the oven to 400 degrees F (200 degrees C).

2

Cut the top off of the head of garlic and place on a piece of aluminum foil. Drizzle with oil and wrap up.

3

Roast in the preheated oven for 25 minutes.

4

Meanwhile, bring a large pot of lightly salted water to a boil. Cook spaghetti in the boiling water, stirring occasionally, until tender yet firm to the bite, about 12 minutes. Drain and set aside.

5

Place tomatoes on a rimmed baking sheet. Drizzle with olive oil and season with salt and pepper.

6

Roast in the oven with garlic for 20 minutes more.

7

Remove from the oven and let cool until safe to handle, 10 to 20 minutes. Place tomatoes in a large bowl and squeeze roasted garlic onto tomatoes. Mash using a potato masher into a sauce.

8

Add spaghetti to sauce; mix well and top with mozzarella cheese and basil. Season with salt and pepper.

NUTRITION FACTS:

519 calories; protein 29.6g; carbohydrates 65.6g; fat 15.2g;

Southwestern Vegetarian Pasta

Prep:

10 mins

Cook:

20 mins

Total:

30 mins

Servings:

6

Yield:

6 servings

INGREDIENTS:

1 tablespoon vegetable oil

1 onion, chopped

½ green bell pepper, diced

2 cloves garlic, chopped

2 tablespoons chili powder

1 teaspoon ground cumin

1 (28 ounce) can diced tomatoes with juice

1 (15 ounce) can chickpeas

1 (10 ounce) package frozen corn kernels, thawed

1 (12 ounce) package uncooked elbow macaroni

½ cup shredded cheese

DIRECTIONS:

1

Heat oil in a large, deep skillet. Saute onion, green pepper, garlic, chili powder and cumin. Stir in tomatoes, chickpeas and corn. Reduce heat to low and simmer 15 to 20 minutes, or until thickened and heated through.

2

Meanwhile, bring a large pot of lightly salted water to a boil. Add macaroni and cook for 8 to 10 minutes or until al dente; drain.

3

Combine pasta and sauce. Sprinkle each serving with Monterey Jack cheese.

NUTRITION FACTS:

421 calories; protein 16g; carbohydrates 72.1g; fat 7.9g;

Creamy Vegan Pasta Salad

Prep:
20 mins
Cook:
10 mins
Additional:
1 hr 30 mins
Total:
2 hrs
Servings:
8
Yield:
8 servings

INGREDIENTS:

½ cup vegan mayonnaise
3 teaspoons white vinegar
1 ½ teaspoons Dijon mustard
½ teaspoon white sugar (Optional)
¼ teaspoon salt
¼ teaspoon ground black pepper
2 cups whole-wheat elbow pasta
½ bell pepper, diced
⅓ cup corn
1 stalk celery, diced
2 tablespoons diced red onion

DIRECTIONS:

1

Bring a large pot of lightly salted water to a boil. Cook elbow macaroni in the boiling water, stirring occasionally, until tender yet firm to the bite, about 8 minutes. Strain pasta and rinse under cold water. Drain.

2

Combine bell pepper, corn, celery, and red onion in a bowl. Mix together vegan mayo, vinegar, Dijon mustard, sugar, salt, and pepper in a small bowl; pour over vegetables. Mix in cold pasta and toss to combine. Taste and adjust seasonings as needed.

3

Cover pasta salad and let cool in fridge for at least 90 minutes before serving, stirring occasionally to mix sauce into pasta evenly.

NUTRITITION FACTS:

180 calories; protein 4.1g; carbohydrates 25.2g; fat 7.5g;

Creamy Pesto Pasta with Almond Breeze

Prep:
20 mins
Cook:
25 mins
Total:
45 mins
Servings:
6
Yield:
6 servings

INGREDIENTS:

1 (16 ounce) package linguine pasta
2 tablespoons olive oil
2 large shallots, thinly sliced
2 cloves garlic, minced
3 tablespoons all-purpose flour
2 cups Original Unsweetened Almond Breeze Almondmilk
½ lemon, juiced
1 tablespoon nutritional yeast (Optional)
Salt and pepper, to taste
Grated Parmesan cheese, for serving
Chopped fresh basil, for serving

Kale Almond Pesto:

1 small bunch kale, stems removed, roughly chopped
½ cup fresh basil
½ cup olive oil
½ cup roasted salted almonds
½ cup grated Parmesan cheese
2 cloves garlic
1 lemon, zested and juiced
Salt and pepper, to taste

DIRECTIONS:

1
In a Dutch oven or large pasta pot, cook pasta according to package directions. Drain pasta water, rinse and return to pot. Set aside.

2
In a saucepan over medium-low heat, saute shallots and garlic in olive oil until softened and fragrant, about 3 to 4 minutes. Season with a hefty pinch of salt and pepper. Add flour, coating shallot and garlic to start a roux. Slowly pour in Almond Breeze, whisking constantly until smooth, and bring mixture to a simmer. Let cook for an additional 5 to 8 minutes, or until thickened. Add lemon juice and nutritional yeast, and season with salt and pepper, to taste.

3
Transfer to a blender and puree until smooth. Blending will help the sauce thicken.

4
While sauce is cooking, pulse pesto ingredients in a blender or food processor, scraping down the sides with a rubber spatula, until mixture is smooth. Season to taste, and set aside.

5

To finish, combine sauce, 1/2 cup of the kale almond pesto and pasta, and stir until well mixed. Serve on plates or in deep bowls, and garnish with extra Parmesan cheese and basil.

NUTRITION FACTS:

662 calories; protein 20.1g; carbohydrates 75.9g; fat 34.1g;

Creamy Gorgonzola Spinach Pasta

Prep:
5 mins
Cook:
15 mins
Total:
20 mins
Servings:
4
Yield:
4 servings

INGREDIENTS:

2 shallots, minced
1 cup heavy whipping cream
4 cups fresh spinach
½ cup Gorgonzola cheese
salt and freshly ground black pepper to taste
1 (16 ounce) package fusilli pasta
1 ½ tablespoons butter

DIRECTIONS:

1

Bring a large pot of lightly salted water to a boil. Cook fusilli in the boiling water, stirring occasionally, until tender yet firm to the bite, about 12 minutes.

2

In the meantime, melt butter in a skillet over medium heat and cook shallots until soft and translucent, 3 to 5 minutes. Pour in cream and cook until heated through, 3 to 5 minutes. Add spinach and crumble in Gorgonzola cheese. Season with salt and pepper and cook until spinach is wilted and sauce has thickened, about 4 minutes.

3

Drain fusilli and toss with sauce. Serve immediately.

NUTRITION FACTS:

730 calories; protein 21.3g; carbohydrates 88.5g; fat 33.9g;

Vegan Cashew Ricotta

Prep:
10 mins
Additional:
4 hrs
Total:
4 hrs 10 mins
Servings:
8
Yield:
8 servings

INGREDIENTS:

2 tablespoons nutritional yeast
3 cloves garlic
¼ teaspoon salt
2 leaves fresh basil
2 cups raw cashews
4 tablespoons lemon juice
2 tablespoons olive oil

DIRECTIONS:

1

Place cashews into a large container and cover with several inches of cool water; let soak, 3 to 4 hours.

2

Drain cashews and transfer to a food processor. Add lemon juice, olive oil, nutritional yeast, garlic, salt, and basil leaves. Process until thick and smooth, 3 to 4 minutes. Stop to scrape down the sides occasionally.

3

Transfer cashew mixture to an airtight container. Refrigerate for 1 to 2 hours

NUTRITION FACTS:

228 calories; protein 7.3g; carbohydrates 11.9g; fat 18.4g;

Asian Carryout Noodles

Prep:
20 mins
Cook:
30 mins
Total:
50 mins
Servings:
2
Yield:
2 servings

INGREDIENTS:

2 leaves bok choy, diced
¼ cup chicken broth
2 tablespoons dry sherry
1 tablespoon soy sauce
1 ½ tablespoons hoisin sauce
⅛ teaspoon salt
2 green onions, minced
1 (8 ounce) package angel hair pasta
1 teaspoon canola oil
1 teaspoon sesame oil
½ onion, chopped
1 clove garlic, minced
1 skinless, boneless chicken breast half - cut into bite-size pieces
1 tablespoon grated fresh ginger

DIRECTIONS:

1

In a large pot with boiling salted water cook angel hair pasta until al dente. Drain.

2

Meanwhile, in a large nonstick skillet heat canola and sesame oil over medium high heat. Saute onion and garlic until softened. Stir in chopped chicken, and cook until chicken browns and juices run clear. Stir in ginger, bok choy, chicken stock, sherry, soy sauce, and hoisin sauce. Reduce heat, and continue cooking for 10 minutes.

3

Toss pasta with chicken mixture until well coated. Season with salt. Serve warm sprinkled with minced green onions.

NUTRITION FACTS:

499 calories; protein 28.1g; carbohydrates 75.4g; fat 9.2g;

Five Ingredient Pasta Toss

Prep:
8 mins
Cook:
12 mins
Total:
20 mins
Servings:
4
Yield:
4 servings

INGREDIENTS:

8 ounces farfalle (bow tie) pasta
1 (15 ounce) can seasoned small white beans, rinsed and drained
1 (14.5 ounce) can fire-roasted diced tomatoes, with juice
¼ cup chopped fresh basil leaves, or amount to taste
¼ cup extra-virgin olive oil
2 cloves garlic, crushed

DIRECTIONS:

1
Combine the olive oil and garlic in a small bowl. Set aside.

2
Fill a large pot with lightly salted water and bring to a rolling boil over
high heat. Once the water is boiling, stir in the bow tie pasta and
return to a boil. Cook the pasta uncovered, stirring occasionally, until
the pasta has cooked through, but is still firm to the bite, about 12
minutes. Drain well in a colander set in the sink.

3

Place the pasta, beans, tomatoes, basil, and 2 tablespoons of the garlic olive oil in a large bowl; toss gently until combined. Serve the remaining olive oil at the table to drizzle over individual servings.

NUTRITION FACTS:

429 calories; protein 14.6g; carbohydrates 63.7g; fat 15.8g;

Vegan Green Lentil Curry

Prep:

10 mins

Cook:

25 mins

Total:

35 mins

Servings:

3

Yield:

3 servings

INGREDIENTS:

1 tablespoon mild curry powder

2 teaspoons ground cumin

1 teaspoon ground turmeric

1 (14.5 ounce) can diced tomatoes

1 (15 ounce) can cooked green lentils

1 tablespoon cooking oil

1 onion, finely chopped

1 green bell pepper, finely chopped

1 clove garlic, finely chopped

1 tablespoon garam masala

DIRECTIONS:

1

Heat oil in a large skillet over medium-high heat and cook onion, bell pepper, and garlic until soft, about 5 minutes. Stir in garam masala, curry powder, cumin, and turmeric and cook until fragrant, 1 to 2 minutes. Add tomatoes, bring to a simmer, and cook for 5 minutes. Add lentils and stir well. Simmer for 10 minutes, but do not bring to a boil.

NUTRITION FACTS:

273 calories; protein 15.3g; carbohydrates 43.2g; fat 6.5g;

Grilled Flatbread Pizzas with Avocado Pesto

Prep:
25 mins
Cook:
25 mins
Total:
50 mins
Servings:
4
Yield:
4 servings

INGREDIENTS:

Avocado Pesto:
2 tablespoons unsalted pistachios
1 medium avocado, peeled and pitted
2 cups lightly packed fresh basil leaves
2 tablespoons grated Parmesan cheese
3 medium cloves garlic, chopped
½ teaspoon salt
¼ teaspoon pepper
¼ cup olive oil

Flatbread Pizzas:

2 medium ears corn, shucked
2 tablespoons unsalted butter, softened
4 store-bought flatbreads (or naan)
2 tablespoons olive oil
2 cups shredded Gruyere cheese
1 cup sliced fresh mozzarella cheese
½ cup thinly sliced red onions
1 cup arugula
1 pinch Crushed red pepper flakes, for serving
Aluminum Foil

DIRECTIONS:

1

Heat a skillet over medium heat. Add pistachios; cooking, shaking often, until toasted, about 5 minutes.

2

Make the pesto by combining the pistachios, avocado, basil leaves, Parmesan, garlic, salt and pepper in a blender. Pulse until the mixture is roughly chopped and then with the blender running, slowly stream in 1/4 cup olive oil. Continue blending until the pesto is a thick paste, scraping down the sides of the blender as needed. Set the pesto aside.

3

Preheat the grill for 10 minutes on medium heat. Spread the butter on the corn, then wrap each ear of corn in Reynolds Wrap® Aluminum Foil. Place the corn on the grill, close the lid and grill the corn, turning it frequently until it is tender, 15 to 20 minutes. Unwrap the corn and when cool enough to handle, slice the kernels off the cob.

4

Brush both sides of the flatbreads with 2 tablespoons olive oil and grill them for 1 to 2 minutes on each side to warm them. Remove the flatbreads from the grill and top with the avocado pesto, Gruyere, mozzarella, red onions and corn.

5

Return the flatbreads to the grill, close the lid and grill until the cheese is melted, about 3 minutes.

6

Remove the flatbreads from the grill and transfer them to serving plates. Top the flatbreads with arugula and crushed red pepper flakes (optional) and then slice and serve immediately.

NUTRITION FACTS:

798 calories; protein 35.9g; carbohydrates 34g; fat 63.1g;

Quinoa with Feta, Walnuts, and Dried Cranberries

Prep:
15 mins
Cook:
15 mins
Total:
30 mins
Servings:
6
Yield:
6 servings

INGREDIENTS:

½ cup chopped walnuts
½ cup dried cranberries
⅓ cup crumbled feta cheese
2 cups low-sodium chicken broth
1 cup quinoa

DIRECTIONS:

1

Bring chicken broth and quinoa to a boil in a saucepan. Reduce heat to low, cover, and simmer until quinoa is tender and broth has been absorbed, 15 to 20 minutes. Transfer quinoa to a bowl.

2

Stir walnuts and cranberries through the quinoa; add feta cheese and gently stir.

NUTRITION FACTS:

243 calories; protein 8.6g; carbohydrates 28.6g; fat 11.4g;

Peas and Pesto Pasta Primavera

Prep:
15 mins
Cook:
11 mins
Total:
26 mins
Servings:
8
Yield:
8 servings

INGREDIENTS:

1 (16 ounce) box Penne
3 cups fresh mixed vegetables such as cauliflower, broccoli, carrots
and asparagus, cut into bite-size pieces
1 ½ cups fresh shelled peas
2 (6.3 ounce) Traditional Basil Pesto
¼ cup half-and-half or whole milk
½ cup grated Parmesan cheese

DIRECTIONS:

1

Bring 4 to 6 quarts of water to a rolling boil, add salt to taste and the Penne, and stir gently.

2

Cook pasta according to package directions adding the vegetables and peas for the last 4 minutes of cooking; remove from heat and drain well.

3

Meanwhile, in a large pot bring the Traditional Basil Pesto and half-and-half* to a low simmer.

4

Add pasta to the sauce in pot; heat through.

5

Serve topped with Parmesan cheese.

NUTRITION FACTS:

348 calories; protein 12.6g; carbohydrates 51.2g; fat 11g;

Tasty Potato Tacos

Prep:
15 mins
Cook:
10 mins
Total:
25 mins
Servings:
4
Yield:
8 tacos

INGREDIENTS:

1 (3.25 ounce) package instant mashed potatoes
½ cup diced onions
1 tablespoon vegetable oil
salt and pepper to taste
8 corn tortillas
½ cup vegetable oil for frying, plus more as needed

Garnishes:

Shredded lettuce
Chopped tomatoes
4 tablespoons Shredded Cheddar-Monterey Jack cheese blend
Salsa

285

DIRECTIONS:

1

Prepare mashed potatoes according to package directions.

2

Heat oil in a skillet over medium heat. Sautee diced onions in oil until tender and translucent, 3 to 5 minutes. Add cooked mashed potatoes and season with salt and pepper.

3

Place tortillas on a plate. Heat in microwave until pliable, 15 to 20 seconds.

4

Place 1/4 cup of potato mixture in each tortilla, fold in half and secure each end with toothpicks.

5

Heat oil in a skillet until shimmering. Fry each taco until crispy and golden brown, about 1 minute on each side.

6

Remove toothpicks and top with garnishes.

NUTRITION FACTS:

513 calories; protein 7.3g; carbohydrates 46.7g; fat 34.6g;

Kale Puttanesca

Prep:
25 mins
Cook:
15 mins
Total:
40 mins
Servings:
4
Yield:
4 servings

INGREDIENTS:

1 tablespoon drained capers
1 (2 ounce) can anchovy fillets, drained and quartered
1 cup canned diced tomatoes, undrained
2 cups coarsely chopped kale
1 (4 ounce) can sliced black olives, drained
½ cup grated Parmesan cheese, or to taste
½ (16 ounce) package whole-wheat angel hair pasta
2 tablespoons olive oil
½ large onion, sliced
2 cloves garlic, minced
1 teaspoon red pepper flakes

DIRECTIONS:

1

Bring a large pot of lightly salted water to a boil. Add pasta and cook for 8 to 10 minutes or until al dente; drain.

2

Meanwhile, heat olive oil in a large skillet over medium-high heat. Add onions, garlic, and red pepper flakes. Cook and stir until the onion has softened and begun to turn golden brown, about 5 minutes. Stir in capers, anchovy fillets, and diced tomatoes, and bring to a simmer. Stir in kale, and simmer over medium-low heat until wilted and tender, about 10 minutes.

3

Once the pasta has cooked and been drained, stir into the puttanesca along with the black olives. Toss and sprinkle with grated Parmesan cheese before serving.

NUTRITION FACTS:

361 calories; protein 15.4g; carbohydrates 41.3g; fat 15.6g;

Spinach-Stuffed Acorn Squash

Prep:

20 mins

Cook:

1 hr 24 mins

Additional:

5 mins

Total:

1 hr 49 mins

Servings:

4

Yield:

4 servings

INGREDIENTS:

1 small onion, chopped

4 cloves garlic, minced

1 (10 ounce) package frozen chopped spinach, thawed and squeezed
dry

¾ cup Italian-seasoned bread crumbs

¼ cup grated Parmesan cheese

¼ cup crumbled feta cheese

2 acorn squash, halved and seeded

3 tablespoons butter, melted

2 teaspoons garlic powder

¼ cup olive oil

1 small red bell pepper, chopped

salt and ground black pepper to taste

DIRECTIONS:

1

Preheat oven to 400 degrees F (200 degrees C). Line a baking sheet with aluminum foil.

2

Brush insides of the acorn squash with melted butter. Dust with garlic powder. Place acorn squash halves cut-side up on the baking sheet.

3

Roast in the preheated oven until tender, 50 to 60 minutes.

4

Heat oil in a large skillet over medium-high heat. Cook red bell pepper until tender, about 4 minutes. Stir in onion and cook until softened, 3 to 4 minutes. Reduce heat to medium and add garlic; cook until fragrant, about 2 minutes. Stir in spinach until it turns dark green, about 3 minutes.

5

Stir bread crumbs into the skillet; cook until lightly toasted, 2 to 3 minutes. Remove from heat; add Parmesan cheese. Mix in feta cheese thoroughly. Season mixture with salt and pepper.

6

Fill acorn squash halves with the red bell pepper mixture, mounding it slightly on top.

7

Bake in the preheated oven until evenly browned, 20 to 25 minutes. Cool for 5 minutes before serving.

NUTRITION FACTS:

487 calories; protein 12.8g; carbohydrates 50.1g; fat 28.9g;

Zucchini and Soy Bean Stir Fry

Prep:
20 mins
Cook:
20 mins
Total:
40 mins
Servings:
4
Yield:
4 servings

INGREDIENTS:

1 tablespoon water
2 tablespoons olive oil
1 onion, chopped
1 zucchini, sliced
5 large mushrooms, sliced
1 tablespoon finely chopped garlic
1 ½ tablespoons reduced-sodium teriyaki sauce
2 tablespoons agave nectar
⅓ cup broccoli florets
⅓ cup cauliflower florets
½ cup shelled edamame (green soybeans)
1 large carrot, chopped

DIRECTIONS:

1

Combine broccoli, cauliflower, edamame, carrots, and water in a microwave-safe bowl. Cover with plastic wrap and microwave for 1 minute until vegetables are tender. Set aside.

2

Heat olive oil in a skillet over medium heat; add onion. Cook and stir until onion is softened and beginning to brown, about 10 minutes.

3

Stir cooked broccoli, cauliflower, edamame, carrots, zucchini, mushrooms, and garlic into the pan; cook and stir until vegetables are cooked through, about 5 minutes.

4

Stir in reduced-sodium teriyaki sauce and agave nectar; cook 5 more minutes.

NUTRITION FACTS:

150 calories; protein 3.1g; carbohydrates 20.9g; fat 7.1g;

Sunny Lentils

Prep:
15 mins
Cook:
25 mins
Total:
40 mins
Servings:
4
Yield:
4 1/2-cup servings

INGREDIENTS:

¼ teaspoon curry powder
salt and ground black pepper to taste
1 (15 ounce) can petite diced tomatoes in juice
¾ cup red lentils
2 tablespoons 1 tablespoon olive oil
⅓ cup onion, chopped
⅓ cup chopped green bell pepper
⅓ cup chopped red bell pepper
1 tablespoon minced garlic
½ teaspoon dried tarragon
shredded sweetened coconut
water

DIRECTIONS:

1

Heat olive oil in a large skillet over medium heat. Add onion, green bell pepper, red bell pepper, garlic, tarragon, curry powder, salt, and black pepper; cook and stir until onion is softened, about 5 minutes. Stir in diced tomatoes; bring soup to a simmer.

2

Stir red lentils and coconut into the soup; mix well to combine. Simmer soup, covered, adding water as needed, until lentils are tender, 15 to 20 minutes.

NUTRITION FACTS:

201 calories; protein 10.9g; carbohydrates 28.3g; fat 4.9g;

Green Risotto with Fava Beans

Prep:

30 mins

Cook:

30 mins

Total:

1 hr

Servings:

4

Yield:

4 servings

INGREDIENTS:

1 cup Arborio rice

¼ cup white wine

¼ cup grated Reggiano Parmesan cheese

salt to taste

½ pound fresh, unshelled fava beans

4 cups chicken broth

3 tablespoons butter, divided

1 small onion, finely chopped

DIRECTIONS:

1

Bring a large pot of salted water to a boil. Meanwhile, shell the favas and discard the pods. Boil the favas for 4 minutes, strain and then immediately plunge into ice water. Let cool for 2 minutes then pierce the favas and squeeze them out of their skins. Separate 3/4 of the favas and puree in a food processor.

2

In a separate large saucepan bring the broth to a simmer, and keep it hot. Meanwhile, in another large saucepan over medium heat, melt 1 1/2 tablespoons of the butter and add the onions. Reduce the heat to low and cook for about 5 minutes; do not brown the onions. Add the rice and cook, while stirring, for 2 minutes. Add the wine, increase the heat to medium, and stir constantly. When the wine has been absorbed, add a little of the hot stock. Once the stock is absorbed, add a little more; repeat this process, stirring constantly, until the rice is cooked through.

3

To the cooked rice add the pureed favas, the remaining 1 1/2 tablespoons of butter, the rest of the favas and the cheese. Cook over medium heat, stirring, until the butter and cheese melt and the puree is incorporated evenly. Season with salt.

NUTRITION FACTS:

457 calories; protein 16.5g; carbohydrates 69.5g; fat 11.1g;

CHAPTER 5: SNACK & SIDES RECIPES

Vegetarian Nori Rolls

Prep:
30 mins
Cook:
30 mins
Additional:
1 hr
Total:
2 hrs
Servings:
5
Yield:
5 servings

INGREDIENTS:

2 tablespoons rice vinegar
4 sheets nori seaweed sheets
½ cucumber, julienned
½ avocado, julienned
1 small carrot, julienned

2 cups uncooked short-grain white rice

2 ¼ cups water

¼ cup soy sauce

2 teaspoons honey

1 teaspoon minced garlic

3 ounces firm tofu, cut into 1/2 inch strips

DIRECTIONS:

1

In a large saucepan cover rice with water and let stand for 30 minutes.

2

In a shallow dish combine soy sauce, honey and garlic. In this mixture marinate tofu for at least 30 minutes.

3

Bring water and rice to a boil and then reduce heat; simmer for about 20 minutes, or until thick and sticky. In a large glass bowl combine cooked rice with rice vinegar.

4

Place a sheet of nori on a bamboo mat. Working with wet hands, spread 1/4 of the rice evenly over the nori; leave about 1/2 inch on the top edge of the nori. Place 2 strips of marinated tofu end to end about 1 inch from the bottom. Place 2 strips of cucumber next to the tofu, then avocado and carrot.

5

Roll nori tightly from the bottom, using the mat to help make a tight roll. Seal by moistening with water the 1/2 inch at the top. Repeat with remaining ingredients. Slice with a serrated knife into 1 inch thick slices.

NUTRITION FACTS:

289 calories; protein 8.1g; carbohydrates 53.6g; fat 4.8g;

Cinnamon Roll Popcorn

Prep:
10 mins
Cook:
15 mins
Additional:
10 mins
Total:
35 mins
Servings:
8
Yield:
8 servings

INGREDIENTS:

1 tablespoon ground cinnamon
1 tablespoon vanilla extract
½ teaspoon baking powder
1 cup chopped walnuts (Optional)
8 cups popped popcorn, or more to taste
1 cup brown sugar
½ cup butter
¼ cup corn syrup
¼ teaspoon salt

DIRECTIONS:

1

Preheat oven to 325 degrees F (165 degrees C). Lightly grease a baking sheet.

2

Place popcorn in a large bowl.

3

Combine brown sugar, butter, corn syrup, and salt together in a saucepan; bring to a boil, stirring occasionally. Remove from heat and cool while stirring constantly for 2 minutes.

4

Stir cinnamon, vanilla extract, and baking powder into butter mixture. Pour butter mixture over popcorn and toss to coat. Mix walnuts into popcorn mixture. Spread popcorn in a single layer onto the prepared baking sheet.

5

Bake popcorn in the preheated oven until coating is set, 10 to 12 minutes. Cool slightly before breaking apart.

NUTRITION FACTS:

368 calories; protein 3.4g; carbohydrates 44.1g; fat 21.4g;

Black Bean Hummus without Tahini

Prep:
10 mins
Total:
10 mins
Servings:
8
Yield:
8 servings

INGREDIENTS:

1 tablespoon sesame oil
4 cloves garlic
1 teaspoon ground cumin
¼ teaspoon ground paprika
¼ teaspoon cayenne pepper
1 (15 ounce) can no-salt-added black beans, drained and rinsed
¼ cup fresh cilantro
¼ cup lime juice
1 jalapeno pepper, trimmed and seeded

DIRECTIONS:

1
Combine black beans, cilantro, lime juice, jalapeno pepper, sesame oil, garlic, cumin, paprika, and cayenne pepper in a food processor or blender; blend until smooth.

NUTRITION FACTS:

62 calories; protein 3.1g; carbohydrates 8.8g; fat 1.8g;

Crunchies

Servings:
30
Yield:
2 - 1/2 dozen

INGREDIENTS:

1 cup flaked coconut
1 cup all-purpose flour
1 cup white sugar
2 cups rolled oats
1 tablespoon golden syrup
⅞ cup butter
1 teaspoon baking soda

DIRECTIONS:

1

Boil butter or margarine and syrup together. Add soda. You should end up with a frothy mixture after soda is added. Stir in coconut, flour, sugar, and oats, and stir well. Press mixture lightly into a large baking tray.

2

Bake at 350 degrees F (175 degrees C) for 15 minutes. Cool, and cut into bars.

NUTRITION FACTS:

122 calories; protein 1.3g; carbohydrates 15.3g; fat 6.5g;

Easy Broccoli and Carrot Stir Fry

Prep:

10 mins

Cook:

16 mins

Total:

26 mins

Servings:

5

Yield:

5 cups

INGREDIENTS:

1 teaspoon cornstarch

1 teaspoon chicken bouillon granules, or to taste

salt to taste

2 tablespoons peanut oil

5 ½ cups broccoli florets

1 carrot, thinly sliced

2 teaspoons water

DIRECTIONS:

1

Bring a large pot of lightly salted water to a boil. Add broccoli and cook uncovered until bright green, about 2 minutes. Transfer broccoli to a bowl of ice water using a slotted spoon and immerse for several minutes to stop the cooking process. Drain.

2

Bring water back to a boil in the same large pot; add sliced carrot and cook for 1 minute. Drain.

3

Mix water and cornstarch together in a bowl until smooth. Add chicken granules and salt and mix well.

4

Heat peanut oil in a wok or large skillet over high heat; saute broccoli and carrots for 2 minutes. Add cornstarch mixture; cook and stir until vegetables are coated evenly, 1 to 2 minutes.

NUTRITION FACTS:

90 calories; protein 2.9g; carbohydrates 8.4g; fat 5.8g;

Baked Tofu Spinach Wrap

Prep:

3 mins

Cook:

2 mins

Total:

5 mins

Servings:

2

Yield:

2 wraps

INGREDIENTS:

1 cup fresh baby spinach

1 tablespoon Ranch dressing

1 tablespoon grated Parmesan cheese, or to taste

2 (10 inch) whole wheat tortillas

1 (7.5 ounce) package hickory flavor baked tofu

½ cup shredded sharp Cheddar cheese

DIRECTIONS:

1

Place the tortillas side by side on a paper plate. Slice tofu, and place slices down the center of each tortilla. Sprinkle cheese over the tofu. Cover with a damp paper towel, and heat in the microwave for about 45 seconds, or until cheese is melted.

2

Pile some spinach onto each tortilla, and pour on some Ranch dressing. Sprinkle with Parmesan cheese, roll tortillas around the filling, and eat.

NUTRITION FACTS:

449 calories; protein 35.2g; carbohydrates 33.9g; fat 20.4g;

Maple Glazed Butternut Squash

Prep:
10 mins
Cook:
20 mins
Total:
30 mins
Servings:
4
Yield:
4 servings

INGREDIENTS:

¼ cup maple syrup
¼ cup dark rum
¼ teaspoon ground nutmeg
1 butternut squash - peeled, seeded, quartered, and cut into 1/2-inch
slices
⅔ cup water

DIRECTIONS:

1
Combine butternut squash, water, maple syrup, rum, and nutmeg in a
saucepan; bring to a boil. Reduce heat and simmer, stirring
occasionally, until squash is tender, about 15 minutes.

2

Remove butternut squash from saucepan using a slotted spoon and transfer to a serving dish, reserving liquid in the saucepan. Continue simmering liquid until reduced and thickened, 5 to 10 minutes; pour over butternut squash.

NUTRITION FACTS:
201 calories; protein 2.6g; carbohydrates 43.2g; fat 0.4g;

Grilled Tofu Sandwich

Prep:
10 mins
Cook:
5 mins
Total:
15 mins
Servings:
2
Yield:
2 servings

INGREDIENTS:

1 tomato, sliced
4 slices firm tofu
1 dash soy sauce
1 pinch salt
2 pita bread rounds
3 tablespoons mayonnaise
3 tablespoons tahini (sesame-seed paste)

DIRECTIONS:

1
Preheat your oven's broiler.

2

Split the pita breads in half so that you have 4 round pieces. Spread mayonnaise on one half of each one, and tahini on the other half. Place tomato slices onto the mayonnaise halves, and sprinkle with a pinch of salt. Place 2 slices of tofu onto the tahini halves, and sprinkle a few drops of soy sauce over. Place the open sandwiches on a large baking sheet.

3

Broil in the preheated oven until hot and bread is slightly toasted, about 4 minutes. Close the halves of each sandwich together, and cut into wedges to serve.

NUTRITION FACTS:
549 calories; protein 19.5g; carbohydrates 44g; fat 34.9g;

Tasty Crispy Baby Potatoes

Prep:
10 mins
Cook:
25 mins
Total:
35 mins
Servings:
4
Yield:
4 servings

INGREDIENTS:

½ teaspoon dried parsley
¼ teaspoon garlic powder
salt and ground black pepper to taste
1 tablespoon olive oil, or more as needed
1 ½ pounds baby potatoes, halved

DIRECTIONS:

1

Place a steamer insert into a saucepan and fill with water to just below the bottom of the steamer. Bring water to a boil. Add potatoes, cover, and steam until just fork tender, about 10 minutes or longer, depending on the size of the potatoes.

2

Transfer potatoes to a bowl. Add parsley, garlic powder, salt, and pepper; toss to coat.

3

Heat oil in a large skillet over medium-high heat. Add potatoes to the hot oil. Cook, shaking the skillet occasionally, until potatoes are browned on all sides, about 10 minutes.

NUTRITION FACTS:

162 calories; protein 3.5g; carbohydrates 29.9g; fat 3.5g;

Pickled Daikon Radish and Carrot

Prep:
20 mins
Additional:
5 hrs
Total:
5 hrs 20 mins
Servings:
4
Yield:
4 servings

INGREDIENTS:

1 small carrot, peeled and cut into matchsticks
1 daikon radish, peeled and cut into matchsticks
2 tablespoons chopped fresh cilantro
1 Thai chile pepper, seeded and chopped
½ cup distilled white vinegar
¼ cup white sugar

DIRECTIONS:

1

Heat vinegar and sugar in a saucepan over low heat until sugar is
dissolved. Remove from heat, and refrigerate to cool. Place daikon and
carrot in a glass jar with the cilantro and chile peppers. Pour the
cooled vinegar mixture over, submerging the vegetables. Cover and
refrigerate for at least 4 hours, or overnight.

NUTRITION FACTS:

70 calories; protein 0.7g; carbohydrates 17.2g; fat 0.1g;

Tofu and Rice Stuffed Peppers

Prep:
25 mins
Cook:
1 hr 10 mins
Total:
1 hr 35 mins
Servings:
4
Yield:
4 servings

INGREDIENTS:

1 ¾ cups marinara sauce, divided
salt to taste
ground black pepper to taste
2 red bell peppers, halved and seeded
2 orange bell peppers, halved and seeded
2 cups shredded mozzarella cheese
8 slices tomato 1 cup uncooked brown rice
2 cups water
2 tablespoons olive oil
1 clove garlic, minced
1 (12 ounce) package extra-firm tofu, drained and diced

DIRECTIONS:

1

Place rice and water in a pot and bring to a boil. Cover, reduce heat to low, and simmer 45 minutes, or until tender.

2

Heat the olive oil in a skillet over medium heat, and stir in garlic and tofu. Cook about 5 minutes. Mix in 1/4 cup marinara sauce, season with salt and pepper, and continue to cook and stir until tofu is evenly brown.

3

Preheat oven to 350 degrees F (175 degrees C).

4

Using a wooden spoon or spatula, press an equal amount of rice into each pepper half. Layer rice with remaining marinara sauce, and 1/2 the cheese. Press equal amounts of tofu into the pepper halves. Place 1 tomato slice on each pepper, and top peppers with remaining mozzarella. Arrange stuffed peppers in a baking dish.

5

Bake 25 minutes in the preheated oven, until cheese is melted. Serve 1/2 of each color pepper to each person.

NUTRITION FACTS:

554 calories; protein 28.5g; carbohydrates 56.1g; fat 25g;

Baked Potato Chip Nachos

Prep:
10 mins
Cook:
20 mins
Total:
30 mins
Servings:
6
Yield:
6 servings

INGREDIENTS:

1 tablespoon salt
1 cup shredded Cheddar cheese
 6 potatoes, peeled and thinly sliced
2 tablespoons olive oil

DIRECTIONS:

1
Preheat oven to 425 degrees F (220 degrees C). Line a rimmed baking
sheet with parchment paper.

2
Spread potato slices out on baking sheet. Coat with olive oil and salt.

3
Bake potatoes in the preheated oven until tops are golden and edges
are crispy, 15 to 20 minutes.

4

Layer baked potatoes with Cheddar cheese; continue baking until cheese is melted, 5 to 10 minutes.

NUTRITION FACTS:

280 calories; protein 9g; carbohydrates 37.5g; fat 10.9g;

Broccoli Cauliflower Pepita Salad

Prep:
15 mins
Additional:
1 hr
Total:
1 hr 15 mins
Servings:
10
Yield:
10 servings

INGREDIENTS:

½ cup light mayonnaise
½ cup plain nonfat Greek yogurt
2 tablespoons red wine vinegar
2 tablespoons coconut palm sugar
1 teaspoon Dijon mustard
½ teaspoon salt
3 cups coarsely diced broccoli
3 cups coarsely diced cauliflower
1 red bell pepper, diced
½ cup diced onion
½ cup shelled roasted pumpkin seeds (pepitas)

DIRECTIONS:

1

Mix broccoli, cauliflower, red bell pepper, onion, and pumpkin seeds in a large bowl.

2

Whisk mayonnaise, yogurt, red wine vinegar, palm sugar, Dijon mustard, and salt together in a separate bowl; drizzle over the broccoli mixture and toss to coat.

3

Cover bowl with plastic wrap and refrigerate 1 to 2 hours before serving.

NUTRITION FACTS:

125 calories; protein 3.9g; carbohydrates 10.4g; fat 8.3g;

Brussels Sprout Slaw with Cranberries

Prep:
15 mins
Total:
15 mins
Servings:
12
Yield:
12 servings

INGREDIENTS:

⅓ cup canola oil
¼ cup apple cider vinegar
1 tablespoon celery seed
salt and ground black pepper to taste
5 ounces dried cranberries
1 pound Brussels sprouts, shredded
4 carrots, peeled and shredded
1 cup shredded red cabbage
1 cup creamy salad dressing
1 cup mayonnaise

DIRECTIONS:

1

Combine Brussels sprouts, carrots, and cabbage in a large bowl.
Combine salad dressing, mayonnaise, canola oil, vinegar, celery seed,
salt, and pepper in a separate bowl. Pour dressing over vegetables and
toss well to combine. Add dried cranberries and toss again

NUTRITION FACTS:

313 calories; protein 1.8g; carbohydrates 19.3g; fat 26.4g;

Flax Seed Crackers

Prep:
20 mins
Cook:
3 hrs
Additional:
8 hrs
Total:
11 hrs 20 mins
Servings:
8
Yield:
32 crackers

INGREDIENTS:

¼ teaspoon garlic powder
¼ teaspoon onion powder
1 pinch cayenne pepper
1 cup raw flax seeds
¾ teaspoon salt
1 cup cold water

DIRECTIONS:

1

Place flax seeds in mixing bowl. Add salt, garlic powder, onion powder, and cayenne. Pour in water. Stir. Cover with plastic wrap. Refrigerate overnight.

2

Preheat oven to 200 degrees F (95 degrees C). Line a rimmed baking sheeting with a silicone mat or parchment.

3

Transfer soaked flax seeds to prepared baking sheet. Spread out into a thin, flat rectangle, about 1/8 inch thick, using a spatula. Score the rectangle into about 32 small, rectangles.

4

Bake in preheated oven until flax seeds have darkened and contracted slightly, about 3 hours. Cool in oven with door ajar. Break into individual crackers.

NUTRITION FACTS:

104 calories; protein 3.6g; carbohydrates 5.7g; fat 8.2g;

Tempeh Fajitas

Prep:
10 mins
Cook:
15 mins
Total:
25 mins
Servings:
4
Yield:
4 servings

INGREDIENTS:

1 (4.5 ounce) can sliced mushrooms, drained
½ cup frozen chopped spinach, thawed and drained
1 tablespoon chopped green chile peppers
1 tablespoon chopped fresh cilantro
1 tablespoon dried minced onion
2 tablespoons corn oil
1 (8 ounce) package tempeh, broken into bite-sized pieces
2 tablespoons soy sauce
1 tablespoon lime juice
1 ½ cups chopped green bell pepper

DIRECTIONS:

1

Heat oil in a large skillet over medium heat. Saute tempeh with soy sauce and lime juice until tempeh browns. Stir in bell peppers, mushrooms, spinach, chile peppers, cilantro and dried onion.

2

Increase heat to medium-high and cook until fluids have reduced, stirring occasionally.

NUTRITION FACTS:

207 calories; protein 12.8g; carbohydrates 13.2g; fat 13.3g;

Maple Glazed Carrots

Prep:
10 mins
Cook:
20 mins
Total:
30 mins
Servings:
8
Yield:
8 servings

INGREDIENTS:

⅓ cup maple syrup
salt and ground black pepper to taste
1 ½ pounds baby carrots
¼ cup butter

DIRECTIONS:

1
Place carrots into a pot and cover with salted water; bring to a boil.
Reduce heat to medium-low and simmer until tender, 15 to 20
minutes. Drain and transfer carrots to a serving bowl.

2
Melt butter in a saucepan over medium-low heat. Stir maple syrup into
melted butter and cook until warmed, 1 to 2 more minutes. Pour
butter-maple syrup over carrots and toss to coat; season with salt and
pepper.

NUTRITION FACTS:

120 calories; protein 0.9g; carbohydrates 17g; fat 6g;

Tempeh Sandwiches

Prep:
10 mins
Cook:
20 mins
Total:
30 mins
Servings:
4
Yield:
4 sandwiches

INGREDIENTS:

1 small onion, thinly sliced

1 medium green bell pepper, thinly sliced

1 jalapeno pepper, sliced

2 pita breads, cut in half

soy mayonnaise

1 tablespoon sesame oil

1 (8 ounce) package tempeh, sliced into thin strips

2 tablespoons liquid amino acid supplement

1 tablespoon sesame oil

4 thin slices Swiss cheese

DIRECTIONS:

1

Heat the oil in a large skillet over medium heat. Add the tempeh slices and cook 3 to 4 minutes, or until they start to brown. Pour in half of the liquid aminos and cook for 1 minute. Flip the tempeh slices and cook until toasted, 3 to 4 more minutes. Pour in the remaining liquid aminos and cook for 1 minute. Remove the tempeh, and set it aside.

2

In the same skillet, heat the remaining oil over medium heat. Cook the onion, green pepper, and jalapeno until the vegetables have softened, 4 to 5 minutes.

3

Spread each pita half with 1 teaspoon soy mayonnaise. Stuff each pita with several slices of tempeh, peppers and onions, and a piece of Swiss cheese. Toast the sandwiches in a toaster oven for 2 minutes or until the cheese has melted.

NUTRITION FACTS:

392 calories; protein 21.7g; carbohydrates 24.4g; fat 24.8g;

Vegetarian Bean Burritos

Prep:

15 mins

Cook:

5 mins

Total:

20 mins

Servings:

8

Yield:

8 servings

INGREDIENTS:

2 tablespoons taco seasoning mix, or more to taste

8 flour tortillas

2 cups shredded lettuce

2 cups grated Colby Jack cheese

 1 (15.5 ounce) can pinto beans, drained

2 tablespoons tomato sauce

DIRECTIONS:

1

Blend pinto beans, tomato sauce, and taco seasoning in a food processor until a paste forms.

2

Cook and stir pinto bean mixture in a skillet over medium heat until warmed, about 5 minutes.

3

Place tortillas on a plate and heat in microwave on high until warm, about 30 seconds. Spread warm pinto bean mixture, shredded lettuce, and Colby Jack cheese onto each warm tortilla. Roll the tortilla around the filling to form a burrito.

NUTRITION FACTS:

481 calories; protein 23.5g; carbohydrates 63.6g; fat 15.2g;

Balsamic Bruschetta

Prep:
15 mins
Total:
15 mins
Servings:
8
Yield:
8 servings

INGREDIENTS:

8 roma (plum) tomatoes, diced
1 teaspoon olive oil
¼ teaspoon kosher salt
¼ teaspoon freshly ground black pepper
1 loaf French bread, toasted and sliced
⅓ cup chopped fresh basil
¼ cup shredded Parmesan cheese
2 cloves garlic, minced
1 tablespoon balsamic vinegar

DIRECTIONS:

1

In a bowl, toss together the tomatoes, basil, Parmesan cheese, and garlic. Mix in the balsamic vinegar, olive oil, kosher salt, and pepper. Serve on toasted bread slices.

NUTRITION FACTS:

194 calories; protein 8.3g; carbohydrates 35.2g; fat 2.5g;

CHAPTER 6: DESSERT

Coconut Chocolate Cake

Prep:
15 mins
Cook:
30 mins
Additional:
15 mins
Total:
1 hr
Servings:
16
Yield:
1 - 2 layer 9 inch cake

INGREDIENTS:

25 large marshmallows
1 (14 ounce) package flaked coconut
1 (16 ounce) container prepared chocolate fudge frosting
1 (18.25 ounce) package chocolate fudge cake mix
1 ⅓ cups brewed coffee
2 tablespoons butter
½ cup evaporated milk

DIRECTIONS:

1

Prepare and bake cake mix according to package directions for two 9 inch round pans, except substitute brewed coffee for the water. Cool cakes completely.

2

Make the Filling: In a saucepan over medium heat, combine butter and evaporated milk. Bring to a boil. Add the marshmallows and stir until melted and smooth. Stir in coconut.

3

Assemble the cake: Place bottom layer on serving plate. Spread with entire coconut filling. Cover top and sides with fudge frosting. Refrigerate.

NUTRITION FACTS:

425 calories; protein 3.5g; carbohydrates 63.5g; fat 18.9g;

Drunken Berries

Prep:
15 mins
Cook:
5 mins
Additional:
4 hrs 5 mins
Total:
4 hrs 25 mins
Servings:
8
Yield:
8 servings

INGREDIENTS:

¼ cup pear liqueur
1 pound fresh strawberries, hulled
1 pint blueberries
1 pint fresh blackberries
Original recipe yields 8 servings
Ingredient Checklist
1 ¼ cups white sugar
½ cup water

DIRECTIONS:

1

Combine sugar with water in a saucepan over medium-high heat, stirring until the sugar has dissolved and the mixture comes to a boil. Reduce heat to low and simmer for 5 minutes; remove from heat and let stand 5 more minutes.

2

Stir pear liqueur into the syrup and refrigerate for 1 hour.

3

Gently combine strawberries, blueberries, and blackberries in a large bowl and pour syrup over the berries to coat. Allow berries to stand for about 3 hours to absorb flavors. Mixture can stand up to 3 days if desired.

NUTRITION FACTS:

196 calories; protein 1.2g; carbohydrates 47.3g; fat 0.5g;

Oatmeal Cinnamon Cream Pies

Prep:
30 mins
Cook:
7 mins
Additional:
5 mins
Total:
42 mins
Servings:
30
Yield:
30 cookie sandwiches

INGREDIENTS:

Cookies:

1 ½ cups all-purpose flour
1 teaspoon baking soda
½ teaspoon salt
¼ teaspoon ground cinnamon
1 cup butter
¾ cup dark brown sugar
½ cup white sugar
2 eggs
1 tablespoon molasses
1 teaspoon vanilla extract
1 ½ cups quick-cooking oats

Filling:

2 teaspoons hot water
¼ teaspoon salt
1 (7 ounce) jar marshmallow cream
½ cup shortening
½ cup confectioners' sugar
¾ teaspoon vanilla extract
¼ teaspoon ground cinnamon

DIRECTIONS:

1
Preheat oven to 350 degrees F (175 degrees C). Line 2 baking sheets with parchment paper.

2
Combine flour, baking soda, 1/2 teaspoon salt, and 1/4 teaspoon cinnamon in a bowl.

3
Combine butter, brown sugar, white sugar, eggs, molasses, and 1 teaspoon vanilla extract in a separate bowl; beat with an electric mixer until creamy and smooth. Stir in flour mixture until dough comes together. Stir in oats.

4
Drop cookie dough onto the lined baking sheets, a few inches apart, using a 2-teaspoon cookie scoop.

5
Bake in the preheated oven until edges are starting to brown, 7 to 10 minutes. Transfer to a wire rack to cool completely.

6

Stir hot water and 1/4 teaspoon salt together in a small bowl until salt is dissolved. Let cool, about 5 minutes.

7

Combine marshmallow cream, shortening, confectioners' sugar, 3/4 teaspoon vanilla extract, and 1/4 teaspoon cinnamon in a large bowl; beat with an electric mixer on high speed until fluffy. Mix in cooled salt water.

8

Spread some of the filling on the back of 1 cooled cookie. Add another cookie to form a sandwich. Repeat with remaining filling and cookies.

NUTRITION FACTS:

193 calories; protein 1.7g; carbohydrates 24.1g; fat 10.2g;

Mini Chocolate Hazelnut Cheesecakes

Prep:
30 mins
Cook:
20 mins
Additional:
2 hrs 10 mins
Total:
3 hrs
Servings:
12
Yield:
12 servings

INGREDIENTS:

1 ½ cups crushed chocolate wafers
⅓ cup butter, melted
2 (8 ounce) packages cream cheese, softened
⅓ cup sugar
2 tablespoons Pillsbury BEST® All Purpose Flour
2 large eggs
1 ½ teaspoons vanilla extract
¾ cup Mocha Cappuccino Flavored Hazelnut Spread, divided
1 tablespoon unsweetened cocoa powder

DIRECTIONS:

1

Heat oven to 325 degrees F. Line 12 muffin cups with foil bake cups. Stir crushed wafers and melted butter in medium bowl until evenly moistened. Spoon 2 tablespoons crumb mixture into each bake cup. Press onto bottoms and 1/2 inch up sides of bake cups. Chill 15 minutes.

2

Beat cream cheese, sugar and flour in large bowl with electric mixer on medium speed until fluffy. Add eggs and vanilla, beating just until blended. Remove 2 cups cheesecake filling from bowl; set aside. Add 1/2 cup cappuccino hazelnut spread to remaining cheesecake filling, beating until smooth.

3

Spoon about 1 1/2 tablespoons cappuccino hazelnut filling into each crust. Top evenly with plain cheesecake filling. (Bake cups will be very full.) Bake 16 to 18 minutes or until filling is set. Cool in pan on wire rack 30 minutes. Cover and chill 1 hour or overnight.

4

Remove cheesecakes from pan; remove foil bake cups. Sprinkle surface of cheesecakes with cocoa powder. Place remaining 1/4 cup cappuccino hazelnut spread in small heavy-duty resealable plastic bag. Microwave on HIGH 10 to 15 seconds to soften slightly. Cut very small corner off bottom of bag. Drizzle over cheesecakes.

NUTRITION FACTS:

392 calories; protein 6.1g; carbohydrates 28.5g; fat 28g;

Pistachio Chocolate Checkers

Prep:

50 mins

Cook:

8 mins

Additional:

3 hrs

Total:

3 hrs 58 mins

Servings:

24

Yield:

4 dozen

INGREDIENTS:

1 ½ cups confectioners' sugar

1 cup butter

1 egg

2 ⅔ cups all-purpose flour

¼ teaspoon salt

½ cup finely chopped pistachio nuts

5 drops green food coloring

1 ½ cups confectioners' sugar

1 cup butter

1 egg

2 ⅔ cups all-purpose flour

¼ teaspoon salt

½ cup unsweetened cocoa powder

2 tablespoons milk

DIRECTIONS:

1

To make the chocolate dough, use the first set of ingredients. In a medium bowl, cream together the confectioners' sugar and butter. Stir in the egg. Combine the flour, salt and cocoa, stir into the creamed mixture alternately with the milk. Set aside.

2

To make the pistachio dough, use the second set of ingredients. In a medium bowl, cream together the confectioners' sugar and butter. Stir in the egg. Combine the flour and salt, stir into the creamed mixture. Finally, stir in the pistachios and food coloring.

3

On a lightly floured surface, pat out each dough to a rectangle 6x5 inches. Cut each rectangle crosswise into 8- 3/4 inch strips. Place 1 strip of each color side by side. Place two more strips on top of those, alternating colors. Repeat until the checkerboard is 4 strips high. Use remaining strips to form a second rectangle. Wrap rectangles and refrigerate at least 2 hours, or until firm.

4

Preheat oven to 375 degrees F (190 degrees C).

5

Unwrap the dough and slice crosswise into 1/4 inch slices. Place 1 inch apart on an ungreased cookie sheet.

6

Bake for 8 to 10 minutes in the preheated oven, or until set. Remove cookies from baking sheet to cool on wire racks.

NUTRITION FACTS:

321 calories; protein 4.5g; carbohydrates 37.9g; fat 17.5g;

Hazelnut Cookies

Prep:
20 mins
Cook:
15 mins
Total:
35 mins
Servings:
40
Yield:
40 cookies

INGREDIENTS:

2 teaspoons vanilla extract
2 cups flour
1 teaspoon baking powder
½ teaspoon salt
½ cup chopped hazelnuts
1 cup butter, at room temperature
½ cup white sugar
½ cup packed brown sugar
1 large egg

DIRECTIONS:

1

Preheat the oven to 350 degrees F (175 degrees C). Line a baking sheet with parchment paper.

2

Cream butter, white sugar, and brown sugar together in a large bowl using an electric mixer. Add egg and vanilla extract and beat until well combined. Mix flour, baking powder, and salt in a separate bowl and mix into egg mixture until just combined. Fold in chopped hazelnuts.

3

Use a tablespoon to cut off little portions of dough; roll them into balls. Place on the prepared baking sheet with room in between.

4

Bake in the preheated oven until lightly browned, 10 to 20 minutes

NUTRITION FACTS:

97 calories; protein 1.1g; carbohydrates 10.3g; fat 5.8g;

Vegan Truffles - Toasted Coconut

Prep:
20 mins
Cook:
10 mins
Additional:
1 hr
Total:
1 hr 30 mins
Servings:
12
Yield:
12 servings

INGREDIENTS:

2 ¼ cups raw cocoa powder

½ cup cocoa nibs

½ cup agave nectar

2 teaspoons vanilla extract

1 teaspoon salt

1 ¼ cups shredded unsweetened coconut, or to taste, divided

2 cups pitted Medjool dates

1 cup raw almonds

DIRECTIONS:

1

Preheat oven to 350 degrees F (175 degrees C). Spread coconut out on a baking sheet. Line a separate baking sheet with parchment paper.

2

Bake coconut in the preheated oven, stirring occasionally, until golden and toasted, about 7 minutes.

3

Blend dates and almonds together in a food processor until smooth; add cocoa powder and process until completely incorporated. Transfer date mixture to a bowl.

4

Fold 1 cup toasted coconut, cocoa nibs, agave nectar, vanilla extract, and salt into date mixture until truffle dough is evenly mixed. Roll dough into tablespoon-size balls.

5

Pour remaining toasted coconut into a shallow bowl. Roll truffle balls in toasted coconut to coat; place coated truffles on the parchment-lined baking sheet. Refrigerate truffles until hardened, about 1 hour.

NUTRITION FACTS:

337 calories; protein 7.3g; carbohydrates 50.1g; fat 17.4g;

Raspberry Cup Cakes

Prep:
15 mins
Additional:
5 hrs
Total:
5 hrs 15 mins
Servings:
12
Yield:
12 cupcakes

INGREDIENTS:

¾ cup fresh raspberries, crushed
½ (8 ounce) package cream cheese
10 ½ fluid ounces sweetened condensed
¾ cup graham cracker crumbs
¼ cup chopped pecans
3 tablespoons butter, melted
milk
1 cup frozen whipped topping, thawed

DIRECTIONS:

1

Line a 12 cup muffin pan with paper cup liners. In a medium bowl, combine graham cracker crumbs, crushed pecans and melted margarine, mixing well to blend. Spoon mixture evenly into a 12 cup muffin pan lined with paper cup liners. Press mixture with a spoon to firm bottom. Puree raspberries and set aside.

2

Beat cream cheese until fluffy. Add condensed milk and 1/2 cup of the raspberry puree and mix until well blended. Fold in whipped topping.

3

Spoon evenly into baking cups. Freeze for at least 5 hours. When ready to serve, remove paper liners. Invert cakes onto individual serving plates. Drizzle remaining raspberry puree over cakes. Garnish with a few whole raspberries. Serve frozen.

NUTRITION FACTS:

227 calories; protein 4.1g; carbohydrates 25.1g; fat 12.8g;

Cranberry Cashew Jumbles

Prep:
30 mins
Cook:
10 mins
Additional:
30 mins
Total:
1 hr 10 mins
Servings:
48
Yield:
48 cookies

INGREDIENTS:

1 egg
2 teaspoons grated orange zest, or more to taste
1 teaspoon vanilla extract
1 cup chopped salted cashews
1 (6 ounce) package dried cranberries, chopped
1 ½ cups confectioners' sugar
3 tablespoons orange juice
2 cups unbleached all-purpose flour
¾ teaspoon baking powder
¼ teaspoon baking soda
1 cup packed light brown sugar
½ cup butter, softened
½ cup sour cream

DIRECTIONS:

1

Preheat oven to 375 degrees F (190 degrees C). Line baking sheets with parchment paper.

2

Whisk flour, baking powder, and baking soda together in a bowl.

3

Beat brown sugar and butter together in a bowl using an electric mixer on medium speed until smooth and creamy; add sour cream, egg, orange zest and vanilla extract and beat until well mixed. Stir flour mixture into brown sugar mixture until dough is smooth. Fold cashews and cranberries into dough; drop by rounded teaspoons, 2-inches apart, onto prepared baking sheets.

4

Bake in the preheated oven until lightly browned, 10 to 12 minutes. Cool on the pans for 10 minutes before removing to cool completely on a wire rack.

5

Whisk confectioners' sugar and orange juice together in a bowl until glaze is smooth. Drizzle glaze over cookies.

NUTRITION FACTS:

103 calories; protein 1.2g; carbohydrates 16.5g; fat 3.9g;

Coconut Tarts

Prep:
15 mins
Cook:
20 mins
Additional:
30 mins
Total:
1 hr 5 mins
Servings:
12
Yield:
12 mini tarts

INGREDIENTS:

1 egg
2 teaspoons evaporated milk
1 teaspoon vanilla extract
1 cup flaked coconut
12 (2 inch) frozen mini tart shells
¼ cup melted butter
¼ cup white sugar
2 tablespoons strawberry jam

DIRECTIONS:

1

Preheat oven to 375 degrees F (190 degrees C). Place frozen mini tart shells on a baking sheet.

2

Beat the butter, sugar, egg, evaporated milk, and vanilla extract, mixing until fully combined. Stir in the coconut. Place 1/2 teaspoon of jam into each mini tart shell, and fill the shells with about 1 tablespoon of the coconut mixture.

3

Bake in the preheated oven until the shells and topping are lightly golden brown, about 20 minutes. Cool on wire rack.

NUTRITION FACTS:

220 calories; protein 2.6g; carbohydrates 24.9g; fat 12.3g;

Zucchini-Chocolate Chip Muffins

Prep:
15 mins
Cook:
20 mins
Additional:
15 mins
Total:
50 mins
Servings:
12
Yield:
12 servings

INGREDIENTS:

1 egg, lightly beaten
½ cup vegetable oil
¼ cup milk
1 tablespoon lemon juice
1 teaspoon vanilla extract
1 cup shredded zucchini
½ cup miniature semisweet
1 ½ cups all-purpose flour
¾ cup white sugar
1 teaspoon baking soda
1 teaspoon ground cinnamon
½ teaspoon salt
chocolate chips
½ cup chopped walnuts

DIRECTIONS:

1

Preheat oven to 350 degrees F (175 degrees C). Grease 12 muffin cups, or line with paper muffin liners.

2

Combine flour, sugar, baking soda, cinnamon, and salt in a large bowl. Mix egg, oil, milk, lemon juice, and vanilla extract in a bowl; stir into dry ingredients until just moistened. Fold in zucchini, chocolate chips, and walnuts. Fill prepared muffin cups 2/3 full.

3

Bake in preheated oven until a toothpick inserted into the center of a muffin comes out clean, 20 to 25 minutes.

NUTRITION FACTS:

265 calories; protein 3.5g; carbohydrates 30.6g; fat 15.2g;

Canadian Maple Rice Pudding

Prep:
5 mins
Cook:
40 mins
Total:
45 mins
Servings:
5
Yield:
5 servings

INGREDIENTS:

½ cup white sugar
½ teaspoon ground nutmeg
½ teaspoon ground cinnamon
1 pinch ground cloves
1 tablespoon butter
¾ cup uncooked short-grain white rice
1 ½ cups water
2 cups 2% milk
1 teaspoon maple flavored extract

DIRECTIONS:

1

Combine the rice and water in a saucepan over medium heat. Bring to a boil, and let simmer over low heat for 20 minutes, or until all of the water has been absorbed.

2

Stir in 1 3/4 cups of the milk, sugar and maple flavoring, bring to a boil, and let simmer over medium heat until thick and creamy, about 15 minutes. Stir in the remaining milk, nutmeg, cinnamon, cloves and butter. Cook stirring over low heat for another 5 minutes. Pour into a casserole dish, or serving bowls, and let stand for 5 minutes before serving. This can be served cold also.

NUTRITION FACTS:

259 calories; protein 5.2g; carbohydrates 48.9g; fat 4.5g;

Poppy Seed Cookies

Servings:
18
Yield:
3 dozen

INGREDIENTS:

2 tablespoons plain yogurt
1 ½ teaspoons orange zest
2 ½ cups all-purpose flour
½ teaspoon baking powder
1 cup shortening
¾ cup white sugar
1 egg
¼ cup poppy seeds

DIRECTIONS:

1

In a medium bowl, cream the shortening and sugar together until fluffy. Stir in the egg, poppy seeds, yogurt and orange zest. Sift the flour and baking powder together; mix into the creamed mixture. Divide dough into 3 portions, wrap in plastic, and chill overnight.

2

Preheat oven to 350 degrees F (175 degrees C).

3

Cut dough logs into 1/4-inch slices. Place circles onto an unprepared cookie sheet and bake for 8 to 10 minutes in the preheated oven. Transfer cookies to wire racks to cool.

NUTRITION FACTS:

211 calories; protein 2.5g; carbohydrates 22.2g; fat 12.7g;

Peanut Butter Snack Bars

Prep:
20 mins
Cook:
10 mins
Additional:
30 mins
Total:
1 hr
Servings:
24
Yield:
24 bars

INGREDIENTS:

parchment paper
cooking spray
¾ cup chopped dark chocolate
½ teaspoon kosher salt
½ cup honey
½ cup creamy peanut butter
¼ cup brown sugar
2 tablespoons agave nectar
1 tablespoon canola oil
¼ teaspoon ground cinnamon
1 teaspoon vanilla extract

2 cups rolled oats

¼ cup wheat germ

¼ cup flax seeds

1 cup crispy rice cereal

1 cup cornflake crumbs

¾ cup chopped smoke-flavored almonds

DIRECTIONS:

1

Line a 9x13-inch baking dish with parchment paper and spray with cooking spray. Spread chocolate evenly over prepared baking dish.

2

Toast oats, wheat germ, and flax seed in a non-stick skillet over medium heat, stirring frequently until oats are lightly golden and fragrant, about 5 minutes. Transfer oat mixture to a large bowl and stir in crispy rice cereal, cornflake crumbs, almonds, and salt.

3

Heat honey, peanut butter, brown sugar, agave nectar, canola oil, and cinnamon in a saucepan over medium heat. Cook and stir until mixture begins to bubble, 3 to 5 minutes. Remove from heat and stir in vanilla extract. Pour peanut butter mixture over cereal mixture; gently stir until well mixed.

4

Spread peanut butter-cereal mixture into the baking dish. Place another sheet of parchment over the mixture and firmly press into the dish until even. Allow to completely cool before removing from baking dish and slicing.

NUTRITION FACTS:

172 calories; protein 4g; carbohydrates 24.8g; fat 7.5g;

Tropical Strawberry

Prep:
10 mins
Total:
10 mins
Servings:
4
Yield:
4 servings

INGREDIENTS:

1 ½ cups yogurt
2 tablespoons white sugar
1 cup crushed ice
1 ½ cups frozen strawberries
1 cup frozen pineapple chunks
½ cup milk

DIRECTIONS:

1

In a blender, blend the strawberries, pineapple, milk, yogurt, sugar, and ice until smooth.

NUTRITION FACTS:

179 calories; protein 6.4g; carbohydrates 35.3g; fat 2.2g;

Banana Oatmeal Raisin Pudding

Prep:
10 mins
Cook:
10 mins
Total:
20 mins
Servings:
4
Yield:
2 cups

INGREDIENTS:

1 tablespoon cornstarch
1 large banana, cut into 1/2-inch slices
⅓ cup raisins
1 tablespoon butter
2 cups milk
½ cup ground oats
⅓ cup white sugar
1 egg

DIRECTIONS:

1

Whisk milk, oats, sugar, egg, and cornstarch together in a saucepan over medium heat; add banana and raisins. Cook, stirring constantly, until pudding is thick, 10 to 15 minutes. Remove from heat and stir in butter. Spoon pudding into dessert dishes.

NUTRITION FACTS:

293 calories; protein 7.9g; carbohydrates 50.9g; fat 7.8g;

Coconut Flour Chocolate Brownies

Prep:
10 mins
Cook:
40 mins
Total:
50 mins
Servings:
12
Yield:
12 brownies

INGREDIENTS:

1 cup white sugar
½ teaspoon salt
½ teaspoon vanilla extract
½ cup coconut flour, sifted
1 tablespoon semisweet chocolate chips, or more to taste
½ cup cocoa powder
⅓ cup virgin coconut oil
6 eggs

DIRECTIONS:

1

Preheat oven to 350 degrees F (175 degrees C). Grease an 8x8-inch baking dish.

2

Stir cocoa powder and coconut oil together in a saucepan over low heat until coconut oil has melted, about 5 minutes. Remove from heat and let cool.

3

Beat eggs, sugar, salt, and vanilla extract together in a bowl; stir in cocoa mixture. Whisk coconut flour into egg mixture until there are no lumps. Pour batter into prepared baking dish; sprinkle chocolate chips over top.

4

Bake in preheated oven until a toothpick inserted into the center come out clean, about 35 minutes.

NUTRITION FACTS:

162 calories; protein 3.5g; carbohydrates 19.3g; fat 9.2g;

Plum Sauce

Prep:
5 mins
Cook:
15 mins
Total:
20 mins
Servings:
10
Yield:
10 servings

INGREDIENTS:

1 tablespoon dried minced onion
1 teaspoon crushed red pepper flakes
1 clove garlic, minced
½ teaspoon ground ginger
¾ (16 ounce) jar plum jam
2 tablespoons vinegar
1 tablespoon brown sugar

DIRECTIONS:

1

In a saucepan over medium heat, combine jam, vinegar, brown sugar, dried onion, red pepper, garlic and ginger. Bring to a boil, stirring. Remove from heat.

NUTRITION FACTS:

102 calories; protein 0.2g; carbohydrates 25.1g; fat 0.1g;

Chocolate Peanut Butter Brownies

Prep:

15 mins

Cook:

20 mins

Additional:

10 mins

Total:

45 mins

Servings:

20

Yield:

20 brownies

INGREDIENTS:

½ cup butter, softened

½ cup peanut butter

½ cup white sugar

½ cup brown sugar

1 egg

1 teaspoon vanilla extract

1 cup all-purpose flour

½ teaspoon baking soda

⅔ cup confectioners' sugar

¼ cup shortening

½ cup milk

1 teaspoon vanilla extract

¾ cup frozen whipped topping, thawed

1 pinch salt

½ cup milk chocolate chips

⅔ cup peanut butter

DIRECTIONS:

1

Preheat the oven to 325 degrees F (165 degrees C). Grease a 9x9 inch baking pan.

2

In a medium bowl, blend together the butter, 1/2 cup peanut butter, white sugar, brown sugar, egg and 1 teaspoon of vanilla until smooth. Combine the flour, baking soda and salt; stir into the sugar mixture. Spread evenly into the prepared pan.

3

Bake for 20 minutes in the preheated oven, until firm. Remove from the oven and sprinkle with chocolate chips. Let stand for a minute, then spread the chips to form a layer.

4

To make the topping, blend together the 2/3 cup peanut butter, confectioners' sugar and shortening. Gradually stir in the milk and 1 teaspoon vanilla. Gently mix in the whipped topping. Chill. When brownies and topping are both cooled, spread topping onto brownies and cut into bars.

NUTRITION FACTS:

262 calories; protein 5.3g; carbohydrates 23.8g; fat 17.3g;

Chocolate-Hazelnut Thumbprints

Prep:
20 mins
Cook:
14 mins
Additional:
30 mins
Total:
1 hr 4 mins
Servings:
24
Yield:
24 servings, 2 cookies each

INGREDIENTS:

2 large eggs eggs, separated, divided
1 teaspoon vanilla extract
1 cup chopped hazelnuts
1 (250 g) package PHILADELPHIA Chocolate Brick Cream Cheese, softened
2 cups flour
½ teaspoon MAGIC Baking Powder
1 cup butter, softened
½ cup packed brown sugar

DIRECTIONS:

1

Heat oven to 350 degrees F (175 degrees C).

2

Mix flour and baking powder. Beat butter and sugar in large bowl with mixer until light and fluffy. Blend in egg yolks and vanilla. Gradually beat in flour mixture until blended. Shape into 48 balls, using about 1 tablespoon for each.

3

Beat egg whites lightly. Dip dough balls, 1 at a time, in egg whites, then roll in nuts until evenly coated. Place 1 inch apart on parchment-covered baking sheets. Press your thumb into centres to indent.

4

Bake 12 to 14 minutes or until edges are golden brown. Cool on baking sheets 5 minutes. Remove to wire racks; cool completely.

5

Spoon cream cheese into pastry bag fitted with star tip. Use to pipe cream cheese onto cookies, adding about 1 teaspoon to each.

NUTRITION FACTS:

188 calories; protein 2.8g; carbohydrates 15.6g; fat 13g

CHAPTER 7: HOMEMADE SAUCE & CONDIMENTS

Vegan Pasta Sauce

Prep:
15 mins
Cook:
20 mins
Total:
35 mins
Servings:
3
Yield:
3 servings

INGREDIENTS:

1 small green bell pepper, diced
½ teaspoon salt
½ teaspoon black pepper
1 teaspoon dried basil leaves
½ teaspoon dried oregano
1 teaspoon vegetable oil
½ small yellow onion, diced
2 cloves garlic, minced
5 large tomatoes, cubed

DIRECTIONS:

1

In a skillet over medium-low heat, saute onion and garlic in the vegetable oil. Place tomatoes into onion and garlic mixture. Stir in diced bell pepper, salt, pepper, basil and oregano. Let simmer for 20 minutes, stirring occasionally. Turn down heat if it starts to stick.

NUTRITION FACTS:

85 calories; protein 3.5g; carbohydrates 16g; fat 2g;

Vegan Queso

Prep:
10 mins
Additional:
5 mins
Total:
15 mins
Servings:
10
Yield:
10 servings

INGREDIENTS:

2 cloves garlic, roughly chopped
1 teaspoon ancho chile powder
1 teaspoon Dijon mustard
¾ teaspoon ground cumin
¾ teaspoon kosher salt
1 cup raw cashews
2 ½ cups hot water, divided
2 tablespoons nutritional yeast
2 tablespoons fresh salsa

DIRECTIONS:

1

Place cashews in a bowl and cover with 1/2 of the hot water. Soak for 5 minutes. Drain.

2

Combine drained cashews, remaining 1 1/4 cup hot water, nutritional yeast, salsa, garlic, ancho chile powder, Dijon mustard, cumin, and salt in a high-powered blender. Start blending at lowest speed and slowly increase the speed. Blend for 2 minutes. Add more hot water if you want the queso to have a pourable consistency.

NUTRITION FACTS:

87 calories; protein 3g; carbohydrates 5.7g; fat 6.5g;

Homemade Vegan Browning Sauce

Prep:
5 mins
Cook:
10 mins
Total:
15 mins
Servings:
20
Yield:
1 1/4 cups

INGREDIENTS:

1 tablespoon reduced-sodium vegetable broth powder
1 teaspoon yeast extract spread
10 tablespoons water
½ cup water
½ cup brown sugar

DIRECTIONS:

1

Heat 1/2 cup water in a saucepan over medium-low heat. Add brown sugar and stir until fully dissolved. Add broth powder and stir until completely combined.

2

Stir in remaining water, 1 tablespoon at a time, stirring constantly until sauce is thick. Simmer, stirring often, until reduced to desired consistency.

NUTRITION FACTS:

23 calories; protein 0.1g; carbohydrates 5.7g;

Vegan Ranch Dressing

Prep:
10 mins
Additional:
4 hrs
Total:
4 hrs 10 mins
Servings:
16
Yield:
2 cups

INGREDIENTS:

2 teaspoons chopped fresh parsley
1 teaspoon garlic powder
1 teaspoon onion powder
½ teaspoon chopped fresh dill
¼ teaspoon ground black pepper
1 ½ cups vegan mayonnaise
2 tablespoons plain soy milk, or as needed
1 tablespoon apple cider vinegar

DIRECTIONS:

1

Mix vegan mayonnaise, soy milk, apple cider vinegar, parsley, garlic powder, onion powder, dill, and black pepper together in a bowl until smooth. Cover with plastic wrap and refrigerate for 4 hours to meld flavors.

NUTRITION FACTS:

104 calories; protein 0.1g; carbohydrates 3.7g; fat 10.1g;

Maple Sriracha Sauce

Prep:
5 mins
Cook:
10 mins
Total:
15 mins
Servings:
20
Yield:
2 1/2 cups

INGREDIENTS:

1 ½ cups maple syrup
¾ cup sriracha sauce
2 tablespoons butter
¼ cup soy sauce

DIRECTIONS:

1
Melt butter in a saucepan over medium heat. Add maple syrup,
sriracha, and soy sauce; whisk together until blended. Simmer until
flavors combine, about 10 minutes.

NUTRITION FACTS:

78 calories; protein 0.2g; carbohydrates 17g; fat 1.2g;

Fantastic Vegan Gravy

Prep:
5 mins
Cook:
10 mins
Total:
15 mins
Servings:
10
Yield:
5 cups

INGREDIENTS:

1 teaspoon lemon juice
1 teaspoon dried basil
½ teaspoon garlic powder
½ teaspoon salt
1 pinch dried rosemary
4 cups water, divided
1 cup cashews
2 ½ tablespoons cornstarch
2 tablespoons soy sauce
2 tablespoons brewers' yeast
2 teaspoons onion powder

DIRECTIONS:

1

Bring 2 1/2 cups water to a boil in a pot. Combine 1 1/4 cups water, cashews, cornstarch, soy sauce, brewers' yeast, onion powder, lemon juice, basil, garlic powder, salt, and rosemary in a blender and process until smooth. Pour mixture into the boiling water in the pot.

2

Use remaining 1/4 cup water to rinse out blender and add to mixture in the pot. Cook gravy until thickened, 5 to 7 minutes.

NUTRITION FACTS:

81 calories; protein 2.6g; carbohydrates 7g; fat 5.2g;

Vegan Lemon-Tahini Dressing

Prep:
10 mins
Total:
10 mins
Servings:
16
Yield:
16 servings

INGREDIENTS:

8 tablespoons tahini
6 cloves garlic cloves, pressed
1 tablespoon coarse salt
1 cup lemon juice
½ cup olive oil

NUTRITION FACTS:

110 calories; protein 1.4g; carbohydrates 3.3g; fat 10.8g;

Coconut Sauce

Prep:
5 mins
Cook:
20 mins
Total:
25 mins
Servings:
10
Yield:
1 1/4 cup

INGREDIENTS:

1 (14 ounce) can coconut milk
1 cup brown sugar

DIRECTIONS:

1

Bring the coconut milk and brown sugar to a boil together in a heavy-bottomed pot. Reduce heat to medium low; cook and stir while boiling until the mixture is thick and the volume has reduced by about half, about 20 minutes.

NUTRITION FACTS:

161 calories; protein 0.8g; carbohydrates 22.7g; fat 8.4g;

Mango Coconut Sauce

Prep:
15 mins
Cook:
10 mins
Total:
25 mins
Servings:
6
Yield:
3 cups

INGREDIENTS:

¾ cup heavy cream
2 tablespoons fresh lime juice
2 mangoes, peeled, pitted, and cut into 1-inch chunks
¾ cup coconut milk

DIRECTIONS:

1

Place the mangoes into a blender, and blend until smooth. Pour the mango puree, coconut milk, heavy cream, and lime juice into a saucepan and blend thoroughly; bring to a boil over medium heat. Serve immediately.

NUTRITION FACTS:

204 calories; protein 1.6g; carbohydrates 13.8g; fat 17.2g;

Fast Vegan Pesto

Prep:
5 mins
Total:
5 mins
Servings:
6
Yield:
6 servings

INGREDIENTS:

2 tablespoons nutritional yeast
2 cloves garlic
½ teaspoon salt
¼ teaspoon ground black pepper
3 cups fresh basil leaves
⅔ cup olive oil
¼ cup pine nuts

DIRECTIONS:

1

Combine basil leaves, olive oil, pine nuts, nutritional yeast, garlic, salt, and black pepper in the bowl of a food processor; pulse until smooth.

NUTRITION FACTS:

259 calories; protein 3.4g; carbohydrates 2.6g; fat 27.1g;

Amazing Cheese Sauce

Prep:
5 mins
Cook:
10 mins
Total:
15 mins
Servings:
4
Yield:
4 servings

INGREDIENTS:

2 cups shredded Cheddar cheese
1 teaspoon salt
½ teaspoon freshly ground black pepper
½ teaspoon cayenne pepper
½ cup butter
¼ cup all-purpose flour
2 cups half-and-half

DIRECTIONS:

1

Melt butter in a saucepan over low heat. Blend in flour and cook until mixture is smooth and bubbly, 2 to 3 minutes. Remove from heat; stir in half-and-half, Cheddar cheese, salt, pepper, and cayenne. Return to heat and cook, stirring constantly, until sauce is smooth, about 5 minutes. Keep warm until serving.

NUTRITION FACTS:

669 calories; protein 21.9g; carbohydrates 12.4g; fat 59.9g;

Creamy Garlic Sauce

Prep:
2 mins
Cook:
5 mins
Total:
7 mins
Servings:
4
Yield:
4 servings

INGREDIENTS:

2 cups heavy cream
1 tablespoon chopped fresh parsley
salt and pepper to taste
2 tablespoons cornstarch
½ cup water, divided
2 tablespoons chopped garlic
1 teaspoon garlic powder

DIRECTIONS:

1

Pour half of the water into a saucepan, and bring to a boil over medium heat. Add the garlic and garlic powder, and boil until the water has almost evaporated, about 5 minutes. Stir in the heavy cream, parsley, salt, and pepper. Mix the cornstarch with the remaining water, and stir into the sauce. Cook, stirring constantly, until thickened, about 3 minutes.

NUTRITION FACTS:

435 calories; protein 2.9g; carbohydrates 8.9g; fat 44.1g;

Japanese Miso and Sesame Sauce

Prep:
5 mins
Total:
5 mins
Servings:
2
Yield:
2 servings

INGREDIENTS:

1 ½ teaspoons minced fresh ginger
1 teaspoon soy sauce
1 teaspoon sesame oil
2 tablespoons mirin (Japanese sweet rice wine)
1 tablespoon miso paste
1 tablespoon ground dried wakame (seaweed)

DIRECTIONS:

1

Mix mirin, miso paste, dried wakame, ginger, soy sauce, and sesame oil together in a bowl until combined.

NUTRITION FACTS:

76 calories; protein 1.5g; carbohydrates 7.6g; fat 2.9g;

Jalapeno Hummus

Prep:
10 mins
Total:
10 mins
Servings:
8
Yield:
8 servings

INGREDIENTS:

2 tablespoons lemon juice
½ teaspoon ground cumin
½ teaspoon curry powder
crushed red pepper to taste
1 cup garbanzo beans
⅓ cup canned jalapeno pepper slices, juice reserved
3 tablespoons tahini
3 cloves garlic, minced

DIRECTIONS:

1
In a blender or food processor, mix the garbanzo beans, jalapeno
peppers and reserved juice, tahini, garlic, and lemon juice. Season with
cumin, curry powder, and crushed red pepper. Blend until smooth.

NUTRITION FACTS:

75 calories; protein 2.6g; carbohydrates 9.1g; fat 3.5g;

Roasted Salsa

Prep:
15 mins
Cook:
40 mins
Additional:
10 mins
Total:
1 hr 5 mins
Servings:
32
Yield:
4 cups

INGREDIENTS:

2 tablespoons chopped fresh cilantro, or more to taste
2 tablespoons cider vinegar, or more to taste
¾ teaspoon dried oregano, or more to taste
¾ teaspoon ground cumin, or more to taste
¾ teaspoon kosher salt, or more to taste
¾ teaspoon ground black pepper, or more to taste
olive oil cooking spray
7 roma tomatoes, halved and cored, or more to taste
2 Anaheim chile peppers, halved lengthwise and seeded
2 jalapeno peppers
1 poblano chile pepper, halved lengthwise and seeded
2 onions, quartered
2 garlic cloves, peeled
1 lime, juiced
½ teaspoon celery salt, or more to taste

DIRECTIONS:

1

Preheat oven to 450 degrees F (230 degrees C). Line a roasting pan or baking sheet with aluminum foil and coat with cooking spray.

2

Arrange tomatoes, cut-side down, in the roasting pan; add Anaheim chile peppers, jalapeno peppers, and poblano peppers, all skin-side up. Add onions and garlic to roasting pan. Spray the vegetable mixture with cooking spray.

3

Roast in the preheated oven until tomato and chile pepper skins are blistered and charred, 40 to 45 minutes. Remove from oven and cool for 10 to 15 minutes, keeping skins on tomatoes and chile peppers.

4

Blend tomato-chile pepper mixture, lime juice, cilantro, cider vinegar, oregano, cumin, kosher salt, black pepper, and celery salt in a food processor using quick pulses until desired consistency is reached. Refrigerate salsa in an air-tight container.

NUTRITION FACTS:

12 calories; protein 0.4g; carbohydrates 2.6g; fat 0.1g;

Garlic Mayonnaise

Prep:
10 mins
Total:
10 mins
Servings:
12
Yield:
1 1/2 cups

INGREDIENTS:

2 egg yolks
1 tablespoon white wine vinegar
1 ¼ cups olive oil
6 cloves garlic
½ teaspoon sea salt

DIRECTIONS:

1

Crush the garlic cloves with the salt into a paste using a mortar and pestle; transfer to a bowl. Stir the egg yolks and vinegar into the mashed garlic. Gradually whisk the olive oil into the mixture in small amounts until the mayonnaise is thick and glossy.

NUTRITION FACTS:

210 calories; protein 0.5g; carbohydrates 0.6g; fat 23.2g;

Vegetarian Gravy

Prep:
10 mins
Cook:
20 mins
Total:
30 mins
Servings:
10
Yield:
2 1/2 cups

INGREDIENTS:

4 teaspoons nutritional yeast
4 tablespoons light soy sauce
2 cups vegetable broth
½ teaspoon dried sage
½ teaspoon salt
¼ teaspoon ground black pepper
½ cup vegetable oil
⅓ cup chopped onion
5 cloves garlic, minced
½ cup all-purpose flour

DIRECTIONS:

1

Heat oil in a medium saucepan over medium heat. Saute onion and garlic until soft and translucent, about 5 minutes. Stir in flour, nutritional yeast, and soy sauce to form a smooth paste. Gradually whisk in the broth. Season with sage, salt, and pepper. Bring to a boil. Reduce heat, and simmer, stirring constantly, for 8 to 10 minutes, or until thickened.

NUTRITION FACTS:

134 calories; protein 1.7g; carbohydrates 6.9g; fat 11.2g;

Enchilada Sauce

Prep:
10 mins
Cook:
30 mins
Total:
40 mins
Servings:
12
Yield:
12 servings

INGREDIENTS:

1 teaspoon ground cumin
¼ teaspoon ground cinnamon
3 tablespoons all-purpose flour
5 tablespoons hot chili powder
4 ½ cups chicken broth
½ (1 ounce) square semisweet chocolate
1 tablespoon vegetable oil
1 cup diced onion
3 tablespoons chopped garlic
1 teaspoon dried oregano

DIRECTIONS:

1

Heat oil in a large saucepan over medium-high high heat. Saute onion until tender. Stir in garlic, oregano, cumin and cinnamon; saute for a few minutes.

2

Stir in flour and chili powder, stirring until sauce thickens. Slowly whisk in chicken broth; reduce until sauce reaches desired consistency. Stir in chocolate until melted and well blended.

NUTRITION FACTS:

43 calories; protein 1g; carbohydrates 6.1g; fat 2.2g;

BBQ Sauce

Prep:
5 mins
Total:
5 mins
Servings:
3
Yield:
3 servings

INGREDIENTS:

½ teaspoon dry mustard
⅛ teaspoon ground white pepper
⅓ cup ketchup
1 teaspoon tamari

DIRECTIONS:

1
Stir ketchup, tamari, mustard, and white pepper together in a bowl

NUTRITION FACTS:

30 calories; protein 0.8g; carbohydrates 7g; fat 0.3g;

Raspberry Sauce

Prep:
10 mins
Cook:
5 mins
Total:
15 mins
Servings:
8
Yield:
2 cups

INGREDIENTS:

2 tablespoons orange juice
2 tablespoons cornstarch
1 cup cold water
1 pint fresh raspberries
¼ cup white sugar

DIRECTIONS:

1

Combine the raspberries, sugar, and orange juice in a saucepan. Whisk the cornstarch into the cold water until smooth. Add the mixture to the saucepan and bring to a boil.

2

Simmer for about 5 minutes, stirring constantly, until the desired consistency is reached. The sauce will thicken further as it cools.

3

Puree the sauce in a blender or with a handheld immersion blender and strain it through a fine sieve. Serve warm or cold. The sauce will keep in the refrigerator for up to two weeks.

NUTRITION FACTS:

53 calories; protein 0.4g; carbohydrates 13g; fat 0.2g;

Baba Ganoush

Prep:
15 mins
Cook:
20 mins
Additional:
30 mins
Total:
1 hr 5 mins
Servings:
4
Yield:
4 servings

INGREDIENTS:

⅛ teaspoon ground cumin
⅛ teaspoon red chile powder
1 tablespoon extra-virgin olive oil
½ tablespoon plain yogurt, or more to taste
salt to taste
1 pound eggplant
2 tablespoons lemon juice
2 tablespoons tahini
2 cloves garlic
1 pinch paprika

DIRECTIONS:

1

Preheat the oven to 450 degrees F (230 degrees C). Lightly oil a baking sheet.

2

Halve eggplants and brush cut sides with olive oil. Place face-down onto the prepared baking sheet.

3

Roast in the preheated oven until softened, 20 to 25 minutes. Remove from oven and let cool, about 30 minutes.

4

Scoop flesh out of skins and place in a mesh strainer. Discard skins. Press down on flesh to remove liquid or drippings. Transfer eggplant flesh to a food processor. Add lemon juice, tahini, garlic, cumin, and chile powder. Drizzle olive oil on top of everything. Blend well, 45 seconds to 1 minute.

5

Mix in plain yogurt and season with salt. Serve with a sprinkle of paprika over top for garnish.

NUTRITION FACTS:

109 calories; protein 2.7g; carbohydrates 9.5g; fat 7.7g;